Duane Vorhees

BETWEEN

HOLOCAUSTS

Hog Press
PO Box 5069
Madison, WI 53705-5069
USA
hogpress.com
editor@hogpress.com
+1 (352) 215-7558

HOG PRESS

BETWEEN HOLOCAUSTS

2024 © Duane Vorhees

All rights reserved. No part of this work covered by the copyright hereon may be reproduced or used in any form or by any means—graphic, electronic, or mechanical, including photocopying, recording, taping, or information storage and retrieval systems—without written permission of the publisher. Neither the author nor the publisher make any representation, express or implied, with regard to the accuracy of the information contained in this book and cannot accept any legal responsibility or liability for any errors or omissions that may be made.

ISBN: 978-1-941892-97-8

x.com/culicidaepress – facebook.com/culicidaepress
threads.net/culicidaepress – instagram.com/culicidaepress

Our books may be purchased in bulk for promotional, educational, and/or business use. Please contact your local bookseller or the Culicidae Press Sales Department at +1-352-215-7558 or by email at sales@culicidaepress.com

Book layout and design © 2024 by polytekton

Table of Contents

HOLOCAUST AND REGENERATION	8
A MIND REWINDS	9
MY FINGERS	10
THE PART IN THE MIDDLE	11
PEOPLE LIVE IN CIRCUMSTANCE	12
ATOLL	14
ZOMBIE VAMPIRE MUMMY….	15
MONTANA MOTEL	16
FURNACE AND FREEZER	17
A FEMINOPHILE'S PLEA	18
THE OBLIGATIONS OF A FREEDMAN	19
SO JENNIFER	20
WE WITHIN THE WHEELS: DALIT	24
EITHER ALZHEIMER'S OR THE LIGHTNING BLAST	26
WHEN THE DAY WAS DARK	27
BORN FOR TWILIGHT	28
THIS INDIFFERENT ETERNITY	29
Narcissus poeticus	30
SIEGE	31
THE DEVOLUTION OF A VAN GOGH SOUL	32
TO MY YOUNG SELF	33
HIGH COUP	34
THE FORGOTTEN HEART	35
NYUN	36
WHAT I DID LEARN	38
CAREFUL DRAGGING	39
THE CONJUGATION OF AGING	40
FORGOT YOUR BODY	41
NIGHT AND DAY	42
THE WALL	43
THE CIRCULAR ARK OF LIFE	44
MY LIFE WAS MAPPED OUT EARLY	45
LOVE'S MEASURE	52
MY TURN TO COME	53

SEER	54
CONVEX CONCAVE SEX	55
FUnowTUwasRE	56
MONUMENT/MYTH	57
AMANUENSIS CUNNILINGUS	58
THE SNAKE IN THE APPLE PRESS:	
COMPETING NOTES FROM LAST NIGHT'S SEX	59
ORDER AND ENGAGEMENTS	61
ESOTERIC	62
APPLE BLUES	63
AND JUST WHEN I THOUGHT THE EARTH WAS TURNING COLD	64
MAGNIFYING GLASS	65
AN ORDINARY LOVE STORY	66
AMAZING FANTASY #16	67
NEEDLES	68
sAVAnnA	69
MY WIFE	70
BETWEEN TWO SUNS	71
YOU SAY I SAY	72
UNLUSTING	73
HOW-TO KAMASUTRA	74
EMPTY AND PEBBLED	76
STILL STRANGERS:	
EROS	
IN EROSION	77
HIGHWAY 14	81
QUATRAINS, EXPLICATION	82
BADGES	83
WHAT YOU WILL	84
VARIETIES OF RELIGIOUS EXPERIENCE	86
SOLEMNITY OF THE ASCENSION: A POEM ARISES	93
INVOCATION	94
POETRIES DOWN AND ACROSS	95
5IVE BY 5IVEs	96
BELLY/MIND	97
LOVERS PREFER ROMANCES BECAUSE	98
THE POETS	99
TAKE ME IN	100
THE SILENCE MAY BE MORE IMPORTANT THAN THE NOISE	101

TATTOO YOU	102
WE LUNATICS LOVE MARBLE POETS	112
ORIGAMI	113
RUBICON	114
THE OBSCURITY OF HEAVEN	115
WHAT ABOUT THE AGE OF LOVERS?	116
UNAPPRECIATED GIFTS	118
TIMES AS GOLDEN CALVES	119
SIGNS	120
FIX	121
… RAW OF THE ROSES …	122
GAZA REDUX	124
TIME MACHINE	126
ARCHITECTURES DECAY	127
THE DANCE: NANCY	128
UNPARALLELED LIVES	131
THE STATE OF THE LAW	142
TRINITY	143
GENETIC MAGI	144
WHERE DO THESE, OUR CASTRATI, GO?	145
CENOZOIC	147
LOOK AT THESE STREETS: THEY'RE MUSIC.	148
SUBURBAN SHOESTORE	149
FOWL WEATHER	150
METAMORPHOSIS	151
NIGHT SHIFT	152
WEATHER REPORT FOR BLIND OPTIMISTS	153
OLD SONGS SUNG AGAIN	154
UNKNOTTED	155
BODY AND SELF	156
SANCTIFIED	157
TOWARDS A SMALL PLOT	158
ON HUMAN ADAPTATION TO HARSH HABITATS	159
HOW TO SUCCEED AT DAIRY FARMING (AND OTHER PURSUITS)	160
THE LANGUAGE I USE ABROAD	161
FIT AND PROPER	162
FISHING WITH A LINGUIST	163
DECREATION	164
WE GAMBLERS OF FATE ARE PLAYED BY THE JUGGLERS OF TIME	165

Books, and Dishes have this Common Fate: there was never any One, of Either of them, that pleas'd All Palates. And, in Truth, it is a Thing as little to be Wishd'd for, as Expected; For, an Universal Applause is at least Two Thirds of a Scandal. So that though I deliver up these Papers to the Press, I invite no Man to the Reading of them: And, whosoever Reads, and Repents; it is his Own Fault. To Conclude, as I made this Composition Principally for my Self, so it agrees exceedingly Well with my Constitution; and yet, if any Man has a Mind to take part with me, he has Free Leave, and Welcome. But, let him Carry this Consideration along with him, that He's a very Unmannerly Guest, that presses upon another Bodies Table, and then Quarrels with his Dinner.

— Sir Roger L'Estrange

HOLOCAUST AND REGENERATION

Fires hibernate in the trees.
The forest flowers,
red and gray,
race through underbrush,
uproot wild life
and humanity.
The burn tattoos the earth.

But growth curls within the rain.
Balmful sky rivers
swell heaven's banks
to soothe scar wounds.
Seeds find footholds
for a newer green.
Creatures settle in.

Havoc hides inside the grain.
Fields uncelibate themselves.
We clear space
to celebrate
to dance to drink
to lure relief
from the caress that grinds.

Wild tunes unsleep from their reeds.
Skins vibrate,
bongos bang,
strings seduce skillful fingers,
whispering poets
suffer rhythmically
into willing ears.

A MIND REWINDS

My psyche is littered with living Its.
Disregarded superegos still whine,
erotic remnants writhe among the crypts.
Od and Ob hiss between young green vines.

Disregarded superegos still whine.
Bony hilltops strain to catch day's first light.
Od and Ob hiss between young green vines,
their bloodguilt insufficiently contrite.

Bony hilltops strain to catch day's first light,
erotic remnants writhe among the crypts,
their bloodguilt insufficiently contrite.
My psyche is littered with living Its.

MY FINGERS

Visit me in my mushroom tower and I will come to you
down this deep dark ditch amid tinder black flowers
down to the buttercups and dew.
My fingers have ridden through the forests of your hair
and slept on belly-gold prairies;
have explored your hidden valleys, climbed snowcapped breasts,
and on your beach hips have rested.
Tanned you naked stand, strata in the earth in layers of
dark
light
dark
light
dark:
while (miners in anticipation) my fingers tremble....

And then it is we who are the layers in the dark, quaking among bedrock,
hardness melting into darkness, joining in new formations,
stalactite buried and unearthed buried unearthed buried unearthed
through the long geologeons of night

till finally separated by a fault

...and our sky becomes snow on coal.

THE PART IN THE MIDDLE

My body is the goblet
that gives shape to the wine
but not its substance
but not the circus within.

The wine owes its spirit
to its soil and sun.

The frames around our portraits
corral us from the world.

Padlocks on our gates
keep time's rustlers from our herd,
rob mustangs of free gait
through an unchanged dirt.

No iceberg remains frozen
in perpetuity.
The whims of fortune
affect its prosperity,
just as its origin
forms its destiny.

Assassins and diplomats
share the same DNA
also the same fate;
circumstance and how it plays
determine how they're cast
and where they are staged.

PEOPLE LIVE IN CIRCUMSTANCE

Prophets
coffin fears.
They undim the years
and make futures clear.
Each instant starts new infinities and we want to learn our world before it leaves and the present in constant process of departure is all of time we possess and we want to change reality we say but won't imagine others until prophetic language speaks itself and inertia is the prophet's strongest weakness.
Poets,
clothed in words,
are philosophers
who live as paupers,
ambassadors of imagination, and their hands acting as mankind's tongues make the machinery that molds humanity and their chisels read our marble's manuscript to free its sheltering angels. The poets' sort of characters presses their texts on the stubborn world's soft tissues.
Healers
seek to cure
the pains of the world,
improve the impure
with powders potions pellets promises prayers prophylactics and prosthetics and redeem the work of their harbinger barbersurgeons, barbarous locks smiths, who balded us while tonsured ones whittled our natures away.
Teachers
reach our minds
by opening blinds
to show us our signs
bright enough to darken our sight, reveal our oceans' icebergs, use their mistakes instincts and stimuli to instruct our eternal youth eager only to grow old.
Scholars
caulk the cracks
in the walls of fact
caused by careless lack
of application as their brains' gray boredom yearns to learn about all the abouts to catalog and diagram and quest to close the gap between the sag of our intellect and the stretch of actuality, but our tired libraries strive for arson because we know when nothing is left all will be understood.

Rulers
view their role
as plugging the holes
in their fated goals
and they deploy their troops their laws their clubs their crusades their mobs and their parades to advance their cause of making the patch of our earth a carpet for their comfortable feet and leave us as shirazless as Shiraz. We say we need rulers to draw our lines straight but the rules rulers impose are intended for us ruled ones only.
Soldiers
know: to kill
they must always drill
and harden their wills
to deform enemy stones into tombs and they expect command and stratagem to stand up their haughty uniforms against opponent motley and bayonet resistant pacifists.
Judges
budge the law
from hammer to saw,
from justice to fraud,
they are the chaste prostitutes who should always be on trial for verdicts that define abstinence as masturbation and we must prepare to wear our loudest scarf to their dockets their gallows and their guillotines.

Prophets live in confusion, poets in fantasy, healers in contagion, teachers in ignorance, scholars in mystery, rulers in entitlement, soldiers in destruction, and judges in wickedness.

ATOLL

Poets before me (how many) have extolled
:melons full melons ripe
:those raspberries (pink&wrinkled) delicate atop your double-dip vanilla sundae
:your slice of peach : your wedge of pie : your pyramid of hot cobbler,
tartsweet juices oozing like fresh tar on the newlylaid I- in August Texas....

but none has ever praised
:the gold and graceful arc of the taut banana—O huntsman's bow before release—
:the strong sweeping scimitar of a Southern Cross bole, bent fullsail,
fruitful coconuts proud unfurled, or the sweetwhitesticky elixer within.

no one has ever
noted for eternity
the coy Thanksgiving yam.

ZOMBIE VAMPIRE MUMMY….

One of us was born to die living,
one of us to live dying.

The one and the one
are one and the same.

And there's one other other,
one for whom
living is dying is living—
each one is one and the same.

As we alternate these ones
we cling, otters, to each other,
to these disparate slices
of our pied kaleidoscopic whole.

MONTANA MOTEL

[and the radio cowboy sings]
Come lay your body down close next to mine,
Sure, yes I'm sure, your husband won't mind.
We're in Montana, and he's in Japan.
So lay your body down. Lay it close next to mine.
Just turn your lamp off, and close down the blinds.
If he came home to find us entwined,
your husband's a good man, he'd understand.
So lay your body down. Lay it close next to mine.

(though i taste the desserts of another's mess,
i still miss the silvered service of your limbs,
i must suppress the appetite of these whims
till again i can dine at the table of your breasts.

who else turns his face from the light to stare at shadows?
who abandons the concert to attend an echo?)

Come lay your body down close next to mine.
Sure, yes I'm sure, your husband won't mind.
Sure, yes I'm sure, your husband won't mind.
Sure, yes I'm sure.... Sure, yes I'm sure....

(asleep beneath the bowers of other tresses,
i do miss the slow flower of your eyes.
but i'll water i guess the garden of her yesses
till i rest in the hollow of your thighs:

is what we learn worth the loss of what we forget?)

Come lie here beside me, pass down the wine,
Sure I am that your husband won't mind:
Needs in Montana can't wait for Japan.
So lay your body down,
Lay your body down, body down. Body next to mine....

FURNACE AND FREEZER

My world is hermaphrodite.
A dimension where moral
coexists with the evil.
It grasps equal opposites.
Down is just as good as up.
Yes, there's gray, but black and white
occupy the selfsame sites.
Oceans are the desert's cups.
A vacuum comprises all.
A freezer and a furnace
work to serve a like purpose.
A dwarf is considered tall.
And your wanton naked face
as expressive as your ass.

A FEMINOPHILE'S PLEA

If you want, get a job, it's fine by me.
Drive the tourist carriage, that's all right,
just so's I can ride your dick box for free.
You want to be a fighter pilot? OK with me,
long's I can fly in your cockpit highspeed.
I don't mind even if you want employment
with the Sanitation Dept. Just let me
work nights in your manhole, okay?

THE OBLIGATIONS OF A FREEDMAN

I'm attentive to the tempest
but ignore the lioness
that hunts from within.

And I fear the inner disease
but yearn to embrace my temptress.
Again and again.

I am more than I am, and less.
I'm self and society.

Illusions of reality
manifest as machines,
not as holograms,

or Self succumbs to anarchy,
freedom enslaves identity.
Chaos is the plan!

Tradition's electricity
depends on historic currents.

One duty of once-observants
is to strengthen the still-fervent
to resist truth's blasts.

Masters of self are the servants
who attend the Now's sacraments
though its moments passed.

SO JENNIFER

1. Her Name Is Jenny and Many a Morn Has Worn Her Face

:daybreaks are harlots all scarlet and huge with rouge and paste.
:some skies all rosy with hosiery (her limbs so prim, so chaste).
:some days hemorrhage like courage at our battleplace.
:other sunrises are sizes too large – whole yards of lace:
silk towns are pretty but cities of silk go wilt and waste.
(So like my Jenny: her any is much; her touch, embrace.)
(There is no middle. A little with her will work long ways.)

:brown coffee mornings come pouring right up from cup to taste.
:all these sunrisings (dawn-icings) – like thieves, they leave no trace.
(So unlike Jenny:
so many a morn has worn her face, so many evenings.
Her leaving goes dim with flimsy haste.)

2. Jennifer in Two Voices

I know why the sky sings the blues – for you, Jenny, for you – atmosphere breaks down and cries. Once the wind must have had your voice: Wind makes my soul rejoice to hear you echo once more. Your precious beauty to preserve, earth freezes to its nerves in ecstasies of ermine. And the waves for you outreach – the sea begs up the beach, hands-&-knees its way in pride. And trees have honored you in gold, red carpet where you rode, jade ceilings and emerald floors — nature's learned your lesson well how to be beautiful: your appearance is your sermon. Across the landscape many-firred, atmosphere breaks down and cries, urges us make love manifold. To hear your echo once more among the creeks and conifers in ecstasies of ermine, in fields of foxes henna-furred – I hands-n-knees my way inside where moist warmth is plentiful. On jade ceilings & emerald floors, raven-eyed/lynx-face Jennifer: Your appearance is your sermon.

I know why the sky sings the blues – for you, Jenny, for you – atmosphere breaks down and cries. (Across the landscape many-firred, atmosphere breaks down and cries,) Once the wind must have had your voice: Wind makes my soul rejoice to hear you echo once more. (urges us make love manifold to hear your echo once more.) Your precious beauty to preserve, earth freezes to its nerves in ecstasies of ermine. (Among the creeks and conifers in ecstasies of ermine,) And the waves for you outreach – the sea begs up the beach, hands-&-knees its way in pride. (In fields of foxes henna-furred – I hands-n-knees my way inside,) And trees have honored you in gold, red carpet where you rode, jade ceilings and emerald floors (where moist warmth is plentiful, on jade ceilings and emerald floors.) — nature's learned your lesson well how to be beautiful: your appearance is your sermon. (Raven-eyed/lynx-face Jennifer: Your appearance is your sermon.)

3. Queen of Denial

So Jennifer you are.

Wrapped in just your thoughts, (and mine too) [*not that you'd notice*] you assume your Mummy pose in bed. Are you sure your heart's hermetic, secure in its canopic jar? Or is it yet in your breast, just beyond sight, cowering still? (And don't forget your nightly negative confession – the world's bad deeds you've never done — all of them – don't miss even one.)

And that kind Registry woman told you, didn't she, as kindly as she kindly could (but in the blameless guilt of your secret vacuum heart, what was it you heard? And how in your soul did it reverberate?) "*Sorry*. This is all we have. This is all the information anyone has. We can't find out *who you are*. We don't know what year you were born. We can't find out where you were born. Nobody knows *who your parents are*, your mother or your father, or why *they didn't want you*. Someone – we don't know who – found you, wrapped in a *ragged, dirty blanket, lying by the side of the road. You were turned over to the authorities and you were sent to the orphanage. And that's all we know. I'm sorry.* I wish we could help you. *Sorry.*" Of course, you knew the whole story already – how could it hurt you now? "Don't touch me," you warn me, as kindly as you kindly can. "If you just leave me alone   [you, too!]   I can handle this by myself." But a single slow tear somehow engineers its hopeless escape down your Alcatraz cheek.

Like a glove on the dresser. lovely warm soft leather, crafted carefully, turned nicely out. Waiting for the proper hand.

Together (*does that word really mean separately alone?*) in bed again. Pickets intent, rapt in their mission, inspecting invisible perimeters. "All lines secure, Sir." No intruder can penetrate. (*friendly, or otherwise*) and there you lie, wrapped around your arms (not *my* arms), world-weary frightened.

So Duane you are.

4. Jen

Not too short, not too thin.
She hid her out within. She never showed her smile,
never revealed her pain.

WE WITHIN THE WHEELS: DALIT

At the temple festival the tables went humming under the cabbage, rice, and melons. The summer sun waning. The baldbearded helium balloons dancing grandly among nubile paper lanterns, buddhas bronze/rotund. Ah, the season it was of Experience Superior – the feelings of love and the perceived reciprocity of love, when, past all balance and sense and generational propriety, exuberant amidst the consuming and consumed, we two, lanternballoon-alike, food and Buddha commingled, music and the truth congealed. That's why your paradox didn't register at the time.
And the Children happy as tadpoles aswim in father's river. And the Children pampered like feathers adrift in mama's balloon.

Now my beauty r e a c h e s   o u t in search of your moist and hidden cottage. (Remember the crisp sunflowers asmoke unkempt against the steep/&damp scampismelly dirt path. Recall the rose-of-sharon labyrinth oft-credited – before and since – as the soul's taoWay, eelslick & serpent straight, into the nirvanic heart of notUnbeing.) Your thatched and pointed little house – it's not where last I fingered its locks. The knobs now I'm told are handled some other where. But even so, blind and blind, my beauty reaches out
reaches   out
my blind beauty reaches
               out into cold and empty vacuum.
And the Children pampered like feathers adrift in mama's balloon, and the Children dappled in shadow ajoy in haughty first light.

Your holy mantra for the season: Iloveyou can't love you. And this rutting neophyte at your knees picked at the koan's echoed contradictions. I angled it in the light, squinting along its crosshairs, but the scope just would not focus. Flash powder applied, I tried to freeze it in its frame. But the quiver could never quite gel. Dusted for prints, but no proper whorl ever emerged to point its finger conclusively. "I love you can't love you." I parsed the riddle into phonemic meaninglessness but the significance never decoded. Affixed onto the acrylic stage for minutest examination, clarity persistently remained at one remove. Until Enlightenment came at last, slowly in a rush. I'd always known you'd go, of course, but not so suddenly. And not so soon. The painful puzzle pieces shuttered into place. And the Children dappled in shadow ajoy in haughty first light, and the Children, dapper as blue jays, agreed in bawdy verdure. I love you can't love you, Clause the first Personal, in classic equipoise with Clause two Cultural. Subject-clause by

Predicate controlled, the halving twins yining and yanging about, plusandminus all at once. The treasured self, forbidden/desired, embraced/abhorred.

(Oh. my fellow anthropologists, take careful note: her heart's harsh judgment was conditioned by decades and millennia of micromacroforming. Metaphorically speaking, as such, I am the incest taboo. In those society eyes, the faggot in the homophobic gym, the nigger in the genepool, the sheep in the unbleating humanfold. In objective terms, and all in econocultural conext of course, her loving me was always the equivalent of fucking a corpse.)

And the Children, dapper as blue jays, agreed in bawdy verdure, and all us Children vampiric taters asleep in God's root cellar.

But the mantramoth, herself addicted, tethered herself to my tormented flame, the cycle doomed to turn and flutter, return and flutter, and flutter away. Return again, again away, covering and recovering the same old ground, rut after rut after rut again.

And koan's mystery deepens. But the Children happy as tadpoles.

EITHER ALZHEIMER'S OR THE LIGHTNING BLAST

Whizzdizzyingly
cruising The Moment,
arrowing past all awareness:
highway,enginewhiine,steeringwheeltrafficWorldsmudginnnng past
while we, preoccupied, reprise Creation,
absorb Eternity and Logos, Eden/Gethsemane, Genesis-Apocalypse
and the Night the Night,
the private bleeding into the general,
and Ouruniverse proxying for ego.
Glorious cosmic fusion in an infinite minute.
      (or so it briefly eternally seems in our infini-tiny microverse)

The ends of love
are but two

:your V8 plunges from the surface
and, crucified like a butterfly in time,
helpless consciousness heightened,
you hover in slowmotion witness
to the juggernaut earth's decay
just as your metal-again grille
begins to embrace solidity

or: doomed foresight eludes
as you rearend that lightless
semi-tru

WHEN THE DAY WAS DARK

My toes were my eyes till sunrise. It's then that the dawn lit beyond where my footprints knew. But the true Isness remained hid like it did when the day was dark. There's no Hark! and no Eureka! I've no law which can explicate how my fate operates, or why there is life, or when time began, where it ends, who I really am, what is scam. That sun is a blimp. It just limps through the confined sky, lets me eye the way of my tracks – all in back, and none move to head off sunset: Daylight-and-shadow's status quo.

BORN FOR TWILIGHT

Today's worlds lose their edge.
Sharp light softens with age.
Silhouettes turn vague.
Color-shapes gray to sludge.
Horizon slides to sky.
I was born for twilight.
My seven senses smudge.

THIS INDIFFERENT ETERNITY

There is not enough dark
though the night is unmooned.
The stars are toomanyed—
skyfull, prickly pennies
instead of ebonstones.

And thus my mood is mocked.
Cosmos ignores despair
and unechoes my cries.

Depression is the stone
that I must bear alone,
its whole weight in my thighs.

Reflections are unmirrored.

Narcissus poeticus

I am not like you other plants.
Fragrance frozen in its hothouse,
my photosynthesis is awry,
Divorced by the bees and the aphids,
spores are embargoed.
I subtract with every season.

SIEGE

The walls I wear withstand
the world's battering rams,
mangonels, and catapults.
The walls I wear protect
against the firm attacks
of your constant sappers' love.

These masks I wear
advertise my identity.
My glass is clear
to disguise my identity.

THE DEVOLUTION OF A VAN GOGH SOUL

My heart sits tarnished
in its rib prison.
The inclement earth
burns under heavens
ashen and barren.
Who erased the stars?

TO MY YOUNG SELF

Your many ghosts haunt these my yellow years,
they still shout because I cannot speak.

The center of your infinity constricts without dimension.
From the start, these, my unstable molecules, made me your atomic traitor.

I bartered your generous energy for degenerate austerity,
your oratorios, your vision, for these parrots and mirrors.
I traded the fire and the wine for diet coke and ash,
your altars of sacrifice for a sepulcher and some artifice.

I was to complete an elusive wholeness but it reduced to incoherent ruins.

Somewhere along the line a promiscuous warrior traded guts
with this riskfree prayer who avoids your fruit for fear of the rot.
Somehow an artful scientist of metaphor
was transformed into this jester of awkward gestures.

Performance has devolved into formula.

Perhaps,
in time,
that I I now condemn
may become
the I I understand.

HIGH COUP

O moon, so distant…
I'm not smokin' in Tokyo,
my poem will not fire.

"Revolution bursts
sunlight on stained stainless steel:
your yolkcolored hair."

Night's vaunted Shakespeare:
just flaccid Little Willie,
cold to geisha stars.

"Neststraw hair – egg's eye
blue – honeyed limbs: trunkhugging
bearcubMe: climbing."

Sake enflames verse
(you say), arouses rhythm, kindles rhymes sublime—

mine (old drunken whore)
fires up unsuccessfully, sucks relentlessly,

till we fall asleep.
And Bashō the monk remains.
Red raw poem limp, still.

THE FORGOTTEN HEART

Dust is the forgotten heart of my cloud,
a child of the earth orphaned in the sky,
a whisper of thunder before it's loud,
an ambition too humble to be proud,
as innocent as fleece before the dye.

Soot is the forgotten heart of my cloud.
No such elevation should be allowed
[they say]
and nothing so lowly should get so high,
a whisper of thunder before it's loud.
Cloud-me may be alone or in a crowd,
my composition ordered or awry.

Smoke is the forgotten heart of my cloud.
This shriveled world is covered by a shroud
that shifts and gathers like unanswered Why?,
a whisper of thunder before it's loud.

I wish you too to live your life unbowed
from your time of youth to the time you die.
Sand is the forgotten heart of a cloud,
a whisper of thunder before it's loud.

NYUN

"When birds
lose their plumes
in the sand,
they can't
glue balloons
to their hands.
They can't fly
so they die."

The years are like so many sweet girls.
They cuddle against the navel in the middle of the night.
They change O they challenge the body
with pain with delight.

But though the waist is gone, its shadow yet remains.
Is this what we needed?
To lie in fields that we seeded
with the sperm of you/and/me?

My skin is a wrinkled up grocery sack,
all the goodies unpacked and eaten long ago.
My erection turned into slush yesterday,
my eyeballs into snow.

But though the face is gone, the halo yet remains.
All the stones unheeded... The skies... The fields....
Back have kneaded into worms, my butterflies.

And the years. And the years: just like the sweet young girls!
Hanging in memory like leather kites,
gaudy garish harsh stabbing neon lights
to mark the passing of fond remembered rites.

But though the voice is gone, its echo yet remains.
Is this what we needed?
To die in fields which receded with the germs of yesterday?

(A toast: Time is a precious necklace bequested upon your birth. As time's beneficiary, you must realize its worth. Though age encircles your throat with its usual yearly pearl, the worth rests in the wearer and not within the jewel.)

The Duane you loved is gone:
There's a Stranger in his skin.
The old duane was younger,
and the new one's bones are thin.
Former laughs reform as coughs.
The change cloud-to-clod begins.

"When birds lose their plumes in the sand,
they can't glue balloons to their hands.
They can't fly so they die."

[nyun is a Korean homonym that means years or floozies]

WHAT I DID LEARN

My mansard roof — its shingles
lost so very long ago.

In Lhasa at Your temple,
at that brave school in Lisbon,
I studied my imago.

My music group's hit singles
stopped so many songs ago.

I've learned my shakes and wrinkles
and still I wait for wisdom.

CAREFUL DRAGGING

I need to be careful dragging these words from their minefields and dungeons, these weighted syllables of assayed worth. They guard against the bludgeons applied by the enemies of my growth.

When I forget how to live, then that's the when when I will start to die.
My fault lines can't fill my rifts, my rainbow vow can't heal my rainfull sky, until When conquers If.

I live in this continuing city of self-mirroring mirrors.
It is the there where I double and split. Other wheres wither into unintended identities.

My face picks its own disguises from among these many costumes and masks I saved to reveal the lies I wield, with my executioner's axe, when I end hindering cries.

Forgotten thought may find a place to hide in the nooks of memory. Experience can be buried alive – amnesia as amnesty – but the ignored remains can never die.

In the act of becoming the mind is not molded by the body; it thinks it is eyes and wings. The who I am is never my what. I'm part of everything.
My brain is inferior to my soul, my chamber is not my heart.
By navigating the oceans of Whole and staying true to the art, tomorrow's ship escapes yesterday's shoals.

Timeless time measures changes.
No stone is a stone until you kick it, and then time rearranges stones into the anchors of a frigate to mark and limit its range.
Time's economist tallies the cockroach, the coelacanth, the centaur, the allosaurus, the ape, and the sloth … and assigns expiry hours.
But I prolong, impersonating ghosts, while time rearranges me. I am what I was and what I was not, but I'm always becoming me. The "mine" is distinct from the "common lot."

And I think I'm almost me.

THE CONJUGATION OF AGING

Years are no series of jumps across gulfs.
We pass through life on a conveyor belt,
paying little notice to the timelets
that pace our course on the running machine.

We only slowly accept we're the guests
of Is, Are, Was, Were, Be, Being, and Been.
Our exercise machine slows then ends
before we realize we've reached the When.

FORGOT YOUR BODY

My saintbernard digs madly and moans.
She can't find where she buried her bone.
The buccaneer always needed maps
"to fuckin' know where m' gold is at."
I forgot your body and your name
and probably I'll forget again
even though you're like any Past-I
who can't be remembered by Now-I.

NIGHT AND DAY

The moon and I
spend our nights
on fish and tequila.

Then dawn comes on
with welcome
oranges in her basket.

At times like this
we cherish
the gifts of our healers

and yet recall
how eager
once for a casket.

THE WALL

On one side, evil
on one side, good.
But I could not always tell
which side was which of the wall
On one side, Devil.
On one side, God.
Sometimes I couldn't distinguish
and sometimes not even wish to.
On one side, David,
one side, Ahab;
in their misuse of royal might
didn't they both behave alike?
On one side Ahab,
on one side David,
putting their passion over prayer
didn't they take what wasn't theirs?
On one side God,
on one side Devil.
That wall less wall than saddle
when both sides I did straddle.
On both sides, good.
On both sides, evil.
Since no differences at all
I just demolish the wall.

THE CIRCULAR ARK OF LIFE

In my young dog years I was petted and beaten
by strange beings who pavloved me to be human.
And then there were those years I was worked like an ass
by far too many bosses made of flint and brass
until I learned to ape them, and then got ahead.
Then I was the one who tigered while others bled
and I upstreamed and I spawned like a steelhead trout.
But eventually I was gorilla'd out.
I'm an old hound now, sprawling on the wooden porch,
just sunning myself among the fleas and the scorch.

MY LIFE WAS MAPPED OUT EARLY

Gen. 4:15

Dad was a tattoo gypsy, going town to town with his ink, his needles, his salves, and me. XXX He knew everything about the tradition, from tebori to flash. But the man who taught me my traid XXXXXXXX trade should not be responsible for my calling.

LOVE

When I was a kid my family was so poor we couldn't afford paper. Dad would leave little memos all over his body, but in the long run that practice proved impractical. Flesh is finite, after all.

WASTE NOT / WANT NOT

Even the roughest first draft needs a great dead of preparation and preplann

MOTHER

Dad told me that my mother fell in love with his art long before she fell in love with him. The needle against her skin aroused her passion, the pain heightened it, and the message that resulted made it permanent. At last, she transferred the process to the producer. And then I happened along. I don't believe I was one of those inevitable tatoo errors. tattoo errors

"FIGHTING FOR YOUR BUSINESS"

I remember Dad standing at intersections, waving his needles and ink packs in the air, trying to sell simple tattoos to motorists stopped at a red light. This was not a successful business model.

PAT

XXXXXXXXXXXXXXXXXXXXXXXXXXXXXXXXXXXXXXXXXXXXXXXXX
XXXXXXXXXXXXXXXXXXXXXXXXXXXXXXXXXXXXXXXXX

"A JOURNEY OF 1,000 MILES"

All's well that ends well. But I know that an effective beginning is important too. As long as I have tablets to write on, I'm determined to keep at it until I get it right.

BORN TO LOSE

What warning should you say to a blueprint you just met? "I don't have any designs on you."

BOB AND BUSTER

Closeted though I may have been by my father's craft, I always knew my true nature. And that relied on writer's, not dermal art, ink.

JOHNNY LOVES VIOLET

Though I am a tattoo artist, I never uncover my body. Not even my face. I guess people find that a little odd.

SEMPER FI

My father, the would-be entrepreneur, once thought if he could stencil ink vaginas on convicts he could make their imprisonment more bearable. Later, when I was older, he chuckled when he told me that his initial research and drafting had been inherently interesting, though it probably distracted him from his professional application. Unfortunately, his clientele was too set in their ways to be receptive to innovation.

IF YOU DON'T WANT TO GET FUCKED UP DON'T FUCK WITH ME

My father's most interesting tattoo idea involved an inchstick, a penis, and a

OPPORNOCKITY TUNES

Most of the work I get paid for is for something elementary and quick. A name. A pairing. A motto. A cross. Hearts (sometimes broken) are a staple. A lightning bolt. A standard repertoire of mottos. The task is usually quite repetitive, quite boring, unless someone desires a memorial in a private place. Even then it depends on the overall attractiveness of the parchment and frame. But every so often I get a request for something more elaborate – a butterfly, a dragon, mountains and surf, maybe a flowery skull with snakes – that's the opportunity I live for. It's the border between craft and artistry.

ADAM

Where does anything actually begin? Isn't there always something that comes before? The Pre-Creation, as it were, the before the before? Should all autobiographies begin with one's first memory of one's ambitions? Accomplishments or intentions? Maybe it should even start before conception. One's begats from Adam on. Or when particular atoms coalesced.

LUCKY 7

I was seven. The madman my father brought home raved constantly about a "bastard's birthright," about murder and betrayal, about risking his very life and sanity to acquire and hide what he called "the Devil's own Nest Egg," And lots of other nonsense to boot.

FOR MY TREASURE BEYOND PRICE

The glint in the stranger's eyes was like lightning, his shouts thunderclaps, as he screamed about the fortune he'd hid out in the desert and how precariously it teetered in his fevered brain. The memory of its location must – must! — somehow be preserved or it would be lost forever. A map was necessary!

MARK + ROSE

What marks my life apart from all others is the collaboration between my father and a lunatic to transform my body into a treasure map. They agreed that, under the stranger's instruction, Dad would indelibly engrave every landmark, every direction, onto the skin of his only son.

MERCATOR MANSON FOREVER

The night that I became a cartographer's wet dream is inked into my memory LIKE A FUCKING TATTOO OF COURSE. YOU FUCKING MORON! YOU

HAVE TO WRITE BETTER THAN THAT IF YOU WANT TO SUCCEED AT THIS GAME. YOU MUST AVOID HACKNEYED SIMILES.

PATIENCE AND PRUDENCE

The madman was nothing if not incoherent and contradictory, but Father persevered despite the many backtrackings and errors. Every time the crazy stranger would forget some vital detail or recover old ground in some different manner, Dad would have to retrace his old steps and modify his growing design. Mistakes multiplied as the mapping got more confused and maze-like.

999

My back filled with lines and smudges, with scratched-in amendments and appendices to the manic mosaic they were making. The marks soon covered my chest as well and then curved up and down and around my arms and legs. They were just about out of complexion parchment, so the final spot was marked on my face. My penis was judged too small and, more importantly, too variable; an index must be consistent or it loses its utility.

GRACE

HOPE

FRANK NESS

The stranger and my father fed each other's insanities as they filled my skin with their mad designs. We all collapsed into an exhausted coma just as the gray horizon began to peach.

WOMEN BEAR CHILDREN, MEN TATTOOS

And as the sun went down Dad woke me up. "Hurry, Son, we need to leave." Our exit was accompanied by the ragged snorts of the sleeping stranger, the designer of my destiny.

CARPE DIEM

When my scarred skin had nearly recovered, my dad and I braved the stranger's desert sun. We had to stop periodically, whenever we got lost, and Dad would strip me of my clothes, turn me around like a naked lathe, examine my armpit for some hidden clue. We searched for a week but never found any of the landmarks etched om my epidermis.

NO PERFECT BEAUTY W/O STRANGENESS IN THE PROPORTION

After we'd abandoned the desert that first time, Dad decided my secret was too valuable to keep on display. He began wrapping me up like a mummy (a broken bone, perhaps?) under my clothes. I began wearing elaborate scarves around my head. I'm sure I would have been forced to wear a burkha if Dad had ever known what a burkha was.

A MAN CAN BE HONEST IN ANY SORT OF SKIN

What an odd pair we were, Father and I. When we went into a strange town, people would see a tall burning prophet and his midget bandaged up like a burn victim. No wonder that business fell off – especially, I guess – when we tried to sell tattoos door to door.

GALATIANS 5: 17

The Devil's Nest Egg never faded from my father's mind. It was more deeply etched than the deepest pattern he'd ever applied. Itself unchangeable, it nevertheless managed to blur my father until I no longer recognized him. The irony, of course, is that my own original identity had been changed beyond recognition. As I grew from a child to an adolescent into a man, my father grew into a stranger himself. The old madman's lightning bolt occupied Dad's eyes, the old thunderclap voiced itself from his own lips, and that transforming night of the bastard's birthright manifested itself again and again when poor Father forced me to undress so he could examine the chart he'd sired.

I'VE GOT MY MOKO WORKING

XXXXXX I often imagined that we were being followed. Eyes were everywhere, fevered, bloodshot, but patient.

TOM

I was returning late at night from an acquisition of needed materials when I was forcibly confronted by a nightmare from my youth. "You know what I want!" hissed the raspy voice from my past. "But why?" I wailed, my heart like a drum. "Your map is worthless! It didn't take us anywhere!" "You fool! I never intended to leave my secrets in the clear for any idiots to read. The desert sun had fried my memory. The details were still fresh, but I knew they would fade. I needed a quipu, a mnemonic device. So I gave your father just enough topography to remind me, me!, of the true proportions, nothing more. And I added false details to confuse you."" What are you going to do with with me now? Kidnap me? Hold me for ransom?" I knew pleading would be worthless, but I hoped to buy some time to find as escape. "Of course not. I have no need for you at all." His teeth flashed, like that long knife I glimpsed in his free hand. "I only need the treasure map you're wearing!"

NO JUDGE BUT GOD

The sharp blade pierced the soft skin. The stranger screamed in pain as the tattoo needle I'd just purchased entered his hand, followed by a pounding blow on his head with the heavy bag full of my trade's apparatus, accompanied by several more needle jabs into his body. I don't know how seriously he was hurt. I didn't stick around long enough to find out.

Dad didn't get supplies that day. I got out of town as quickly as I could and never went back. It was time for me to strike out on my own. I suppose both men, father and stranger, search for me still.

I SPEAK THE BODY ENGLISH

I'm constantly on the move. Even more than when I was with Dad. I still earn my living from the mindless tattoos that people buy on a drunken whim, but I pursue my profession more furtively, in part for the purpose of self-protection, but also to leave my art to posterity. Sometimes people give me the opportunity to create something complicated on their canvas and, unsuspectingly, they actually provide me the parchment for my serialized tattoo novel. When my composition is completed I thoughtfully apply my protective gauze with my stern admonishment not to remove it immediately. By the time they are able to admire their new acquisition I'm long gone.

LOVE LASTS FOREVER, A TATTOO LONGER THAN THAT

I keep a careful record of my work in progress, knowing someday it will be assiduously assembled and collated by future scholars and appreciative literati. But I miss my loving father from Before, and I miss our old free and easy nomad life when my travel was fun and not under the gun.

TATTOOED IN OUR CRADLES WITH THE BELIEFS OF OUR TRIBE

LOVE'S MEASURE

Although I know marble outlasts wax, longevity isn't love's measure,
and I know how to read with pleasure the artists, the crafters, and the hacks.

MY TURN TO COME

Every foot fits your shoe,
your glove can hold any hand.
You share love everywhere.
I await my turn to dance.

SEER

Between the game
and my aim
lust fills the moment.

Your reply's flame
does the same,
fulfills the omen.

CONVEX CONCAVE SEX

manwoman axandcrack shaftinshaft
drillandwell shovelhole malefemale

FUnowTUwasRE

Ecstatic electricity freezes into pulse as biologies become magnets / your eyes lip my cheeks / my koi mouth plumbs your pond / our trunks forest together, organs tromboned by desire fingers / perpetual fleshmachines yinyang existences / masses gasseate / consciousness shrinks to cosmos / our my-your selves merge, we share atoms

we downlings deitize

MONUMENT/MYTH

1. LA FONTAINE MÉDICIS, JARDIN DU LUXEMBOURG

You stroke the stonework
when you come upon the cyclops
and, so, I fountain.

2. ACIS

The bent bronze was crouched.
Your love urged blood into water
and so I fountained.

AMANUENSIS CUNNILINGUS

My tongue is your servant
you keep at your desk
to dictate to fingers
the words from my mind

in praise of your beauty,
in praise of your worth.
If only my body
consisted of tongues.

My tongue is your serpent
you keep for your cleft,
whose electric tingle
wiggles and entwines,

for love and in duty,
and promotes this verse.
If only my body
were made out of tongues.

THE SNAKE IN THE APPLE PRESS: COMPETING NOTES FROM LAST NIGHT'S SEX

the speedboat through the waves / a wand lost in the magic act
the sandbags and the flood / a spoon in a cup
the Mississippi paddle boat / a skiff in the Delta
the scalpel and the organ / an eyedropper for pinkeye
the marble and the slush / an unguent on a bruise
the etcher and the glaze / a sore-throat lozenge
the snowplow through the drift / a branch scratching on glass
the ice pick and the thaw / a nozzle in the fountain
the mountain and the lava / a sputtering candle wick
the exhaust pipe and an oil change/ a bubbler in the fish tank
the corkscrew in the bottle / a hot water warmer in a blanket
the hailstorm on the windowpane / moonbeams on incandescent lamps
the skewer in the marshmallow / another quill in the pillow
the chisel against willow wood / a swab on a blister
the spade in the mulch / a sprinkler on the lawn
the needle in that vein / a hose in the garden
the hammer on the vase / a quarter in the coke machine
the beater and the egg / a spatula amid the frosting
the blade of the blender / a finger in pudding
the antler on the cabin wall / sunglasses over tears

You, oh crane, make the sky.

ORDER AND ENGAGEMENTS

I thought love's inherent anarchy
erodes the institution.
I saw the situation starkly,
imposed my constitution,
and then, to defend love's covenant,
fortified all my redoubts.

But I abandoned my battlements
and witnessed my army's rout.
Too late, enlightenment came darkly;
the armistice was troubling:
I learned no lover's a monarchy,
all lovers are republics.

ESOTERIC

as eager initiates
in lovers' freemasonry,
that true and ancient order,
we are illuminati
of the night's old mysteries

through its well-established rites,
its scripts, shared grasps, finger codes,
its postures, pledges, passwords—
we advance by slow degrees
our prescribed intimacies

APPLE BLUES

Look at me, bald, fat as an apple.
Here I am, bald, fat as an apple.
But don't value goods just by their wrapper.

Old as your father, that's what you said.
"You're old's my father," is what you said.
But that's no bother, ain't decrepit yet.
May look like a wolf, pitted and ugly.
Big bad old wolf, grizzled and ugly.
Feed me love enough, tame as a puppy.

I may be a shit, but I make your garden grow.
You say I'm a shit, I make your garden grow.
When you need a prick, let me be your rose.
Look at me: bald, fat as an apple.
Look at me, bald just like an apple.
Don't value the goods just by their wrapper.

(Lean me against your marrow like a giant midget jumbo shrimp. Hold my poor minute against all infinity like any other parasol you'd prop against a hurricane. A gossamer-armored middleaged scholar in swimming trunks, let my steady frailty hold the frailty of your own, let my cardboard walls withstand the world's assault.)

If you break your compass, I am true north.
You lose direction, here I am, true north.
And when you end your wanders, I'm fire in your hearth.
If I'm silent, don't have much to say.
I'm kind of silent, not a lot to say.
Just like my violence, words left yesterday.

Horny old bastard, last grape on the vine.
Horny old bastard, the end of the line.
Wrinkled and blasted grape a-makes the sweetest wine.

AND JUST WHEN I THOUGHT THE EARTH WAS TURNING COLD

—all the ancient fields of my youth, the sweet meadows
—just when my old shepherd's head was a-going sheeplike itself
—snowy, poor-sighted, far too slow
—then and just then
—that new lamb came into my fold.

And the earth turned over again, and no more old.

MAGNIFYING GLASS

You're just that lens
that focuses that passion
that assembles
that clearing conflagration.

Borders are kept
by habit, time, or treaty.
When virgin lands
are opened to new seeding
planters supplant
foragers, and old hunters
confront lightnings
to experience thunder.

Our species needs union for generation
but it splits to get searchlight approbation.

AN ORDINARY LOVE STORY

If you are the vault, I
am the combination.
(a tux,
a mum,
a candled dinner)
If I am the match, you
are the conflagration.
(a kiss,
the cum,
those tangled
fingers)
If we are the watch, you
are the complication.

AMAZING FANTASY #16

To locate her elongated man,

an invisible girl
hoisted her green lantern.

Her archenemy – that scarlet witch! —

countered with a dark spell
hidden in a shadow

that would blind any moon knight's vision.

But concupiscence stirred
this lightning lad to flash.

Firestorm-sparked, my tinder kindling breached

her lonesome miracle:
I'm now her human torch.

NEEDLES

We wedded the ink with the skin.
The priest performed acupuncture
consecrated by heroin,
and the nurses purled the sutures
while the knitters prepared the syringe.

These rites we practiced unpinned time.
We survived our blessings and sins,
we withstood our charities and crimes.
We know our bricks wither within
but our ivies, they cling, they climb.

sAVAnnA

AblAze WiTh hUnger/disCOVerY
,epiderM AnTs rUn eleCTriC AgAinsT This plAin:
ThrOUgh YOUr CUrlY grAsses These sOfT YellOw liOns
prObe   And Under The ripe VUlTUres in The briAr Trees
MY YOUng ChiMps rOMp UpOn gOlden MOUnds —

O The Wind gloWs WiTh dUsT   & dArK MYsTerY

And O The MOOn hOWls
    AbOVe
        Us And YOUr riVer sWAllOWs mY AArdVArK.

MY WIFE

My wife is the flag
placed on climbers' highest crags.
My wife is the mirror
who patrols my appearance
and makes sure all is fit
and I'm vetted to grace the public.
She's the armorer
who's forged our love and honor.
My wife is the ear
who grants the pre-clearance
for my poems' weight and wit
so they're ready to face the critics.
My wife is that fire
to kindle and quell desire.

BETWEEN TWO SUNS

One more melanoma day
ends itself in ash and cinder.
Our crisp souls, clichéd
to yet another auto-da-fé
of competitive conformity.
But (just now starting)
we mount our nocturnal bucket brigade,
begin passing forth and back
these cool liquids of our life,
refill and back again,
refill and back again
between two suns.

YOU SAY I SAY

You say
your bees come alive
when I prod your hive.

I lift your balloon
and hold you to ground.

I say
I pour and pour ghee
and you absorb me.

UNLUSTING

If your vaginal kindling
stops firing my effigies,
will other environments
break into our quarantine?

The waters of the fountains
have frolicked through every day
while all the time draining back
into the underground's black.

Can proud naked expression
become clothed in words at last?

The unlusting of passion
must soon commence some passage
of a shape into a shadow
when my kisses don't redden
your features any longer.

Today may be eternal
but the yesterday is long.
Yes. the yesterday is long.

HOW-TO KAMASUTRA

How do I love thee? Let me count the ways....
—Elizabeth Barrett Browning

11. You are the axe in the well. It shines then rusts.
15. Because there is a clearing in the woods. Winter sun is iced beer. The short noon lengthens its shadow.
17. By rotating ringmaster, acrobat, lion tamer, and clown. Entertaining the performers keeps the circus alive.
23. We are like a hinged door that swings wildly.
25. By being the wind coaxing the wallflower.
26. Because our tantric nirvanic altar sacrifices the doves and the lambs, the flour and the wine.
28. By eating as much trout as we can while avoiding the hooks.
34. You are like the hand of the tongue, signing in diverse dialects. No tongueless poet can tell the honey from the vinegar.
39. Because, first, each of us must talk to the other's eye and make our halos sparkle. The organ must fit the occupation.
42. Because pleasure's foundation must hold the skyscraper's weight.
46. Because every successful love merchant barters ego for empathy: To exalt the narcissist, one narcissist must appease the other narcissist.
48. Like the crack that makes the kaleidoscope.
50. Because solids grow hollow, and tall beauties shrink to a willow branch but swell again when roots are watered. Fingers harvest the garden's onions, the parsley patch.
53. By being an interpreter of hints into commands. Genitals never blush, never lie.
55. Just as the nomad, mapping from one Alone to another, discovers new silk roads along the way.
57. By having a limb that blooms and buds and becomes sometimes a club.
59. You are the careful steward, partitioning the jewels, the perfume, the spice, and the lace from the placenta and the excrement.
61. By allowing the passion to run free while confining the caution.
63. Because desire is the part of us that touches the parts of others.
66. Through the realization that we fell in love with the other's image of our possibilities. So, be your Mahdi! Establish an infinity in every instant.
69. We are our extremities, all we have for reaching out.
72. Through incessant practice. Even the bunglers of love can learn to be jugglers.
75. Because sex completes a bachelor's halfness and is also the prophet of progeny.

77. My Monaco arms seek to engage your vast Russia passions.
80. Through awareness of eternity's sting. Stars swarm around the hive of our moon but remain balanced: We can release ourselves from our body of death in the knowledge that we carry our own prisons and paroles with us.
82. By not becoming so old as to expect passion or so young as to seek respect.
97. I love thee upon greeting.
98. And at leaving.

EMPTY AND PEBBLED
—Cheops Beach in autumn

Naked we together again run
on our gold dust and pearls
beside the sleeping sea.
The waning sun beads our skin
while the wind smothers our lungs.

Every vagina is exposed,
a messy lagar where the wine is born.
Any penis is Hermetical, closed,
an opaque clarinet.

Today the halves of the hinge
are rusty, stiff, and worn.

These times before,
nipple and prick would respond
to the air the sheen the motion
with alert anticipation.
These times before. But no more.

This is what this fall displays:
our lifetimes are pyramids
infinite at base
inexorable toward the point.

STILL STRANGERS:
EROS
IN EROSION

After years
   of wear, she would sew
with those sharp dead
           beads, new thoughts
    into the threadbare pattern of memory,
and he solder
   his older, darker, thoughts into place....

                            ... Long ago...
they learned to slaughter
    their eager laughter and tear
         their deepest tears out of each's other,
they taught themselves to utilize their exquisite words
       like hamhamhammers and broadswords—
then, their mutual wounds
        they wound all about their lives like poison ivy.
(Each just one more bothersome
     clone to the other...)

But

There had been a time
    ,once,

before the tiny
    mutiny,
when they were still strangers
             to anger,
when they could lie naked,
       sun-baked upon the jurassic sands
or beside the slow hearth,
         unearthing new treasures from their together,

                when, in some safe
                            cafe, their yes
                                        -eyes could swallow entire
their sweet menus
            of Venus
and for many an hour
                pour their love
from lip to mouth like milk from a pitcher to a glass.

                                        But that time passed...

Strangely
   angel-like, two
 naif
waifs
blown
 down,
unable to unwind all the ivy accumulation
 in a rugged wind – they just
    shrugged, unable to face down
      the demons of their facetious selves.

        (This is not simply
                    to imply that they weren't determined.
But, over time, stubborn assiduity becomes undermined,
especially when connubial cement lacks
                    reinforcement.
So, by fragile grapevines, over
            tangled ravines,
the values they were hanging onto
            kept changing.
They were unable to forge a structure anew
            or to forget old collapse.
Neither the heights of their dear science nor
       the weight of alerted conscience,
And not Keats, and certainly
      not Yeats,
   could keep the crevices in their isolate selves
from inventing the devices of their together's undoing.)

             Beached,
they discovered the sea:
     inequal parts nausea and mystery.

Haughty grain bows to scythe

HIGHWAY 14

I never went to Luxor
though we drove once to Rushmore.

We loved the minestrone
we ate in Minnesota
en route to South Dakota.

The skies were paved with zircons
that she said must be diamonds.
And I thought of Ramesses
when we found Orion's Belt,
though eager for Roosevelt,
and Washington and Lincoln,
Crazy Horse and Jefferson
in all their granite glory.

Milky Way spilt through the night
like a Nile through vacant blight.

This Hathor cowboy obsessed
over sphinx and obelisk,
so we detoured off 14
for benben on Silent Guide.
My oracle realized
when we crossed the Bad river
toward the Six Grandfathers
Up West North Down South and East
that our stars weren't carats:
they were our fatal scarabs.

QUATRAINS, EXPLICATION

You kissed me in your garden, and then you tortured me.
I learned in your orchard belief forestalled pardon.
With the heat of parenthood you loved me at once
then suddenly took affront when I ate what was good.
Your day hovered, stern and still after the roosters crowed.
I staggered to the crossroad that led up to the hill.
My sweetest tree lost its leaves, my rose just yielded thorns.
My clothes were raffled and torn by guards who were thieves,
while a thief gave me succor. By comrades unfriended,
my murder unattended but for mother and whore.

It's the gravel in the rattle
the critics listen for,
the riddle at the middle of poetry.
That's the ambiguity
that they adore.

You planted my temptation, knowing I would fail,
then carpentered the nails for my situation.
You were judge and betrayer, prosecutor and crowd,
you, the weaver of my shroud, the author of my prayers.
I was Jesus and Adam, pillars of your temple,
my deaths your staged examples. But I am yet a man.

BADGES

Wedged within your fresh crotch —
this now is all I own.

The pasts are buried bones,
arrowheads,
broken pots
that belonged to other lovers,
to lost cultures.
Wastelands conceal the nests
of their long-gone futures.

Keen time dines on butchers' scraps as well as sweet breasts.
Their pasts are buried bones.

This now is all I own.
Calms punctuate
the storms that chart activity.
We were not and won't be.

Lover –
to this culture we belong,
not others.
Hedges, and not bridges,
decorate these towers.

It's not in our power to swap
campaign badges—
they mark brigade victories.

We were not.
We won't be.

WHAT YOU WILL

You intruded my soul—
the whirlwind
amidst my feathers,
the typhoon
among my waters—

Some might call it love and, some, religion
but I'm satisfied to call it passion.

And then our thread despoiled,
the balloon
discovered fetters,
our garden
became our desert.

Wild/still. Static/ecstatic. Push/and/pull.
Anarchy/enchained. — Call it what you will.

You're my rain when I'm dry

VARIETIES OF RELIGIOUS EXPERIENCE

1. Shape of God Debated

Once, the future shape of god
was subjected to debate
between Simons, one self-sage
and the other dubbed a rock.

One said
that a hermitage
was proper for apostles,
and the other
that brothels
were the fittest
for a sage.

Along with the skies,
the Hawk's wings
lift
human prayers and praise.
But all the tears
are embraced
by the coils of the
Snake.

2. Evangelist

The arch science of religion
taught me to carry lips of mercury.
Now I own a hoard.
I wore a heartfelt tongue of stone
while a student of the science of love
when I learned to starve.

3. Pilgrim

At Lourdes you chose to laugh
at my perfect body.
You mocked me on my knees,
scoffed my alabaster,
scorned my lisp and my limp,
called my cactus lily.
Demanded that I show
sure proof of my disease.
How could you not have seen
the cancers on my skin?
The flags of leprosy?

4. Herbert's Revelations

Ancient George Herbert
—an only poet
known for piety—
when he was dying

was able to put
out another tome,
*Temple: Sacred Poems
and* (it said) *Private*

Ejaculations!!!
Oh, what a volume!
—The hypocrisy
of pious clergy

and their secret sins!
Exposé I sought.
But this was not that.
Just more holy din.

Honest George Herbert,
patient preacher-poet,
proved his piety
even when dying.

5. Neo-Gnostics

The Church of Christ Geographer
fixes its axis
between Bethlehem and Gethsemane,
charts its coordinates at Patmos and at Tarsus.

Heretics infidels schismatics iconoclasts
occupy our incredulous post-pagan planet.

There are those who claim
the universe is actually a Freemasons conspiracy,
and those who maintain
that's absurd – obviously, it's the Rosicrucians.

No, no, some insist
the Universe Machine does exist
but it's a self-construct.

This is in contrast
to those who preach
the universe as a divine wet dream

or, more likely, a component
of a cosmic plan to accomplish
an unfathomable end.
"It's inscrutable!" "It's immutable!" "Oh, it's beautiful!"

(and don't we all admit
the future is finite,
while dreams and gods
are limitless?)

Cosmologists define chaos
as order not yet perceived.

An artist believes
in the mathematical function of the mind:
A poem is a formula.

And every past
is an artifact of imagination;
art, and not religion,
is our only interface
with eternity, with reality.

To those who posit the passing
phenomenologically,
as the present swallowing
some possible tomorrows
to appease the past,

and to those who
pile past upon past
with no diminishment of futures
(though I myself feel yesterdays
lengthen and futures growing short),

the upholders of omnipresence
counter that God is timeless —
God does not believe in Wednesdays —
and the demarcated God
does not admit of territory.

The Church of Christ Geographer
proselytizes its atlas
among us mapless navigators
who lack compass and astrolabe.

6. Limits to Certainty

Compliance with clients and tyrants
has compromised its craft,
but science claims it has no bias
in its pursuit of fact.

Intuition is information
detached from logic's shaft.
Religion is an illustration
but not a photograph;
philosophy, a sly diary
that mixes myth with math.

Knowledge has no certified college
to enlighten our path.

7. The Spirit of Kabbalah

The Cincinnati street tzadik
adjusted his gematria
and fixed his prophylactery.

He cruised the hungry synagogues
in search of that night's disciple,
someone with whom he could invoke
The Seventy-Two Names Of G-d.

In the space between stretch and sag
he worked his oils and amulets,
moved moonlight toward dawn's exit,
and invoked her incantation:

ohgodogodohgodohgod….

8. Triumph and Dirge

You wore beads and visions,
I sported uniforms.
Our clothes were different,
mended at times or torn.

Captured by your angels,
dismissive of my birds,
so driven by Heaven,
unsettled on earth,
you sought Leviathan,
I took care of zebras.

You spoke in prayers and chants
and I in algebra.
A gourmand, a faster,
worldly and holy, we.

Your death:
my disaster, not your catastrophe.

9. Animism

Each wind has a god,
every river, every rock,
and every tree.
There's a god for 11:43.

Though I'm chained, yet I fly

SOLEMNITY OF THE ASCENSION: A POEM ARISES

My tattoo's invisible
though I practice stigmata
and rehearse the rapture.
Epiphany lies quiet.

The show-stopper miracle
auditions first as monster,
but then physics is captured
and gravity stays silent.

INVOCATION

From his temple the Poet said,
"Save these poems in immortal form.
Marked in ink if not carved in stone.
The words are gold, though the type is lead.
May some moroni save the plates
and may my yaksha guard these gates."

POETRIES DOWN AND ACROSS

POETRIES ARE TEMPORARY   mayfly shooting stars.
ETERNITIES LIKE   to take their time.
ROMANCE   is the ordained becoming of my constructive mind.
(INTIMATE   as my private nylon guitar,
CROWSFEET IN THE   wisdoms of my wellworn wrinkles,
SNOW   drifts huddled in my summer hair,
FROZEN FIREWORKS   like answered prayers
PLANTED IN THE   practiced temple-
GARDEN   with a classicist's attentive detail.
AVANT   avant! urges my impatient congregation,
GARDE   garde whispers my hesitant administration's
ANTIQUATED INNOVATION) IS A   knotted coquettish veil,
COMPLICATED AND   confused by vicissitude,
INTRICATE   as a balkan vendetta feud.
SCIENCE THAT   enumerates the course of my moods
SATISFIES   itself with etymology. it ignores
DEMANDING, FICKLE   variations among my lovers and whores.
CLIENTS   of time and romance patronize many stores.

5IVE BY 5IVEs

Within my poet
hides a wild hermit
whose identities
reveal and conceal
themselves, each in turn.

His tongue in my gut
sings and cries and bites.
While never at ease,
it kisses and feels,
it parches and burns.

And then the moans lift
to brain's fingertips,
where they are released.
Then fasts become meals
til monk next hungers.

BELLY/MIND

Sponge draws, stone withstands
inspiration rains.

A formlessness hides
undiscovered forms;
imagination
is the belly's mind.
Stars reign in darkness.

To pay heaven court,
astronomer's scope
always magnifies
observatories.

But when the mind fasts,
it's inspiration
that's the mind's belly.

Palaces empty
without their nobles —
poor indeed are those
whose poems outnumber
their inspirations.

LOVERS PREFER ROMANCES BECAUSE

poets seek to explore "la mer"
while disregarding the isthmus,
and when 'st-stanzas st-stutter
they p-pretend ma-melisma.

THE POETS

The poets are the parents of humanity,
their chroniclers, their museum.
The diluted magics of language
are the dances of the lame,
the pictures of the blind,
the musics of the deaf.

The poets are the link conquerors,
psychoanalytic alchemists.
The auxiliary organs of these prosthetic gods
are the phantom limbs that operate the world.

Poets are the bullets of conformity
and revolution.

The unknowns these beautiful liars advance
become the truths of generations.
Tyrants fashion the heads of their blades
with poets' diamonds.

These apprentices of the machinery of language,
these gibbet masters,
are our lash, our ax, our rack, our crux, our bastinado.

TAKE ME IN

"Take me in." the poet prayed, "take me in." The prophet hid.
"Take me in," the poet said, "take me in."
No banker paid. "Take me in." The soldier fled.
"Sink or swim," the lawyer pled. "Take me in,"
The poet said, "take me in." A woman did.

"Make me warm," the woman cried, "safe from harm."
The poet sighed. "Words are thin," he did reply, "weak and thin.
But yet I'll try. Weak and thin, but yet I'll try."

In the bin by page by page,
in the bin the books were laid,
inch by inch were set ablaze.
Line by line the match was lit.
Word by word
the poems all went.

"Now I'm warm," the woman said,
"safe from harm. But poet's dead."
Poet dead?
Poet dead?
He lives on inside her head.
His words go on inside her head.

THE SILENCE MAY BE MORE IMPORTANT THAN THE NOISE

TATTOO YOU

Embarrassed over the night's activities, the morning blushed into being.

"Lighten up, why don't you?" I said.

***

you got me ticking gonna blow my top

I got to the reception late. An album, an old favorite, was playing in the background. Bruno, the twerp, was already giving his speech. "And so, my associates, together we're about to launch a glorious new chapter in the history of L'INX. Some of you are old friends of the establishment, and some are about to become much closer." But I hadn't come to listen to him anyway. He was just a short fuck with thick glasses and halitosis. An artist, of course, and like all artists he was crazy. So I went to check out Bruno's work or, more precisely, to check out some of the hunks his work adorned. And to take him up on the invitation's offer of a free upgrade. I hoped that meant adding a time-zone adjuster to the working watch he had tattooed onto my wrist.

say what the hell, hang fire

The first likely-looking person I saw was standing at the wet bar, smiling ruefully at the gals who had come to gawk at the job Bruno had done on him. Mike was a high-powered broker with easy access to moneyed clients, he claimed. But he was certainly dressed for this particular occasion, wearing a purple Speedo and expensive sandals. The torso tattooed across his pecs had a toothy green dragon across a man's back, topped by a mop of wild red hair, its legs wrapped around Mike's muscular body, knees at his side, one shapely thigh down the back of his leg and the other around his shoulder.

Mike was just half of a broken set, it seems. His ex had left him long ago, taking with her a similar pattern front and back, except that the figure on her chest looked like Mike would if he were seen from behind. While she would be bouncing on his cock, Mike would be able to see her actual body sprouting like a sunflower toward the ceiling and, simultaneously, a simulacrum of her back hugging his chest; and, their positions reversed, she would have a similar view of him fucking her and embracing her at the same time. And the effect would have been even sexier, I'm sure, had they performed under a full-length ceiling mirror. It would be almost like doing multiple clones! Just the thought was almost enough to make me wet my panties.

don't want to be your slave baby go, baby go, baby go

But when Mike's soul mate stopped mating with him, as he explained in his dull monotone, he still had to carry her corpse on his skin. He was in desperate need of a replacement, but no woman had an appetite for any threesome in which she would be just another slice of rye and Mike's old flame would be the prosciutto in the middle. (Although, looking at his chiseled physique, I admit I was tempted. Briefly, like his Speedo, I suppose.)

But my heart also went out to the old flame. After Mike was gone, it would be bad enough for her to have had a MIKE engraved across her tit forever. But can you imagine what it would be like wearing all of Mike all over her bod when she was trying to make it with Bill or Dave?

"Did I miss anything? The traffic was terrible," I lied. "Just before you came in Bruno was going on and on with some long-winded metaphor about the lines of his newest tattoos being like the circuitry on an advanced computer chip. Wireless, instantaneous communication and control. Some shit like that." I agreed wholeheartedly with Mike's attitude toward long-winded metaphors. "I suppose he was trying to make some point about being connected to his customers through his art, but I couldn't quite understand the imagery. "Would you care for a drink?" Mike motioned to the seat beside him and rambled on. Good luck with that smile, I thought, and withdrew, making a polite excuse about my AA sponsor or something of that nature.

"We've worked hard to design and execute the world's most advanced tattoo art. But the journey, my friends, has just begun. And, as great as the art is – worthy of a Nobel in Skin Design, if there were such a thing – the art is not as important for my future as you, my associates, are. You are the ones who are going to make the future possible." I looked at my inky watch and wondered how much longer the boast would last.

say what a pair, say what a team
we used to ride, ride, ride

Leaving Mike, my attention was drawn to an elderly fellow, in his forties. He wore a face on his tummy that was almost photographic. It was like a portrait of a younger woman that one might see in a museum. Although he was definitely not my type, I walked up to him to congratulate him on his taste in art. But as he pivoted to talk to someone, I saw the oddest design on his back. Beginning at his spine and then curving up to his left shoulder blade and then more gently arcing down toward the crack of his butt was the outline of an ear, or maybe the handle of a loving cup. On the right side of his back was a cryptic message.

J E R
L O
B R E

"I guess beauty is indeed in the eye of the beholder," I thought, puzzled that someone could be so upfront about his traditional taste in art and then, behind his back as it were, be such an ardent Dadaist.

do unto strangers what you do to yourself

I half listened to the drone named Bruno. "I have devoted my whole life to the development of my wonderful new process. And now, it is complete! With your assistance, this revolutionary new method, that combines art and electronics, will change our world! And that is why we are celebrating our great success here today, and why I am extending my offer to augment your earlier tat work, at absolutely no charge." (I thought, Ah! Maybe in addition to getting my watch upgrade I can also get some new tit tats too.)

Chatting with the old guy with the young woman on his chest was a burly fellow I decided I wanted to meet. He was wearing a loose-fitting jacket. Its parka peaked over his head, and a pair of naked legs emerged below the hem. (It made me think, Hmmmm.)

"After I flunked out of clown school – nobody told me I had to read books! — I became a preacher," he said, winking, by way of introduction. He had first come to Bruno to get a little crucifix on his ass, and one thing led to another. And he flipped off his jacket and made a graceful pirouette to show me the extent of what Bruno had done. Both shoulders had huge, black, carefully feathered wings etched across them. A great bird of prey covered the rest of his well-muscled back, its razor talons perched on his calves, its fierce beak and piercing eyes screaming out from the man's bald head. I couldn't help but be a bit frightened by the bird's dramatic pose and wondered how rapturous it would feel to be carried off by such a raptor. It would be like flying, with the man's powerful bulk hovering above me, and I holding his pinions for dear life to keep from falling. Or, actually, to keep falling into his pounding flesh. Just like the poets and the Harlequin romance writers described.

sometimes I wonder why you do these things to me

My reverie was interrupted by the passage through my peripheral vision of someone I thought I'd seen before. Oh yes – she looked like an older version of the woman whose portrait I had admired earlier, the museum piece. As I turned my full attention toward her I noticed her bare midriff. Staring out from it was a younger version of the Old Guy. As unobtrusively as I could, I stole a glance at her back. She too had a huge ear running down one side and strange lettering on the other.

EMY
VES
NDA

Then it dawned on me. Joined together, these two people had perpetuated their young love with an inscrutable private joke permanently carved on their skins, one that nobody else could possibly figure out unless they were standing side by side.

you should leave this small town way behind

I didn't particularly want to talk to her, but I couldn't help but overhear the loud, animated woman she was with talking about "changelings" and "government conspiracies" and "kidnapping rings" and how she had Bruno tattoo bar codes on her whole family so she could always track them and check their identities. I didn't want to talk to her, either, not then, but I made a mental note to try to contact her later. We all need to be vigilant in this world and stay informed.

nothing will stop you, and nothing will stand in your way

"I will, of course, be scheduling all of you for new work in the coming weeks. And tell your friends! For a limited time I will also provide them too with my new-process tattoo art. Gratis."

So, Bruno was, finally, finishing his own remarks and introducing Sam Wise, his star attraction, a local celebrity often featured in the newspapers and on TV. I'm sure everybody in town knew about that man, standing on the platform wearing a posing pouch and nothing else. He was tall enough to play forward in the NBA but built like an NFL tackle, thus providing Bruno a gigantic canvas to work on. And, gradually, over the course of years, and after much planning and consultation, Bruno had turned the behemoth into an Illustrated Tolkien.

"*The Hobbit* and *The Lord of the Rings* both begin and finish at Bag End," Sam told the assembled crowd. "So the patterns begin on both my ankles and both my wrists as well. And the story proceeds up my arms and legs, circling round and round."

He pointed out each geography as he talked. "Mirkwood to Lonely Mountain and Lake Town. Crickhollow to Old Forest to Barrow-downs, to the Inn of the Prancing Pony at Bree. The mines of Moria, Lothlorien. And, of coutse, Mordor!"

He struck a body builder's bulging pose. "Right here," the bicep on his right arm pulsed, "is where Gandalf the Grey escaped from Orthane! And here," his left bicep, "is where he fought with the Balrog and became Gandalf the White! And here," he indicated the vaccination scar on his arm, "right here is where Bilbo got stabbed with the Morgul-blade! And, of course, we have the different adventures as the Fellowship breaks apart in all directions, but the narratives meet up again at Rivendell," his sternum, "and here, in the Misty Mountains" – his butt cheeks jiggled, and we all laughed. (I giggled.)

"And, believe me, Bruno has vividly realized all the characters. Shelob, Aragorn, Legolas, Gimli. The Witch King and the Ringwraiths, Gollum and Sauron. Tom Bombadill. Ents and orcs. You name 'em, they're all here somewhere."

He christened his left armpit Parth Galen and proudly pointed to a sad but noble visage there with gray remorseful eyes. And so Sam went on and on, marvelous though I didn't know half of what he was talking about. The sight of his massive, graceful, multicolored, almost naked body was enough to keep my attention intact. I whispered silent prayers of thanks to the imagination that conceived Middle-earth and to the giant who had now spared me the trouble of reading the books. (Too many! I thought. And too long!)

—Until Bruno, the fuck, interrupted, thus breaking the spell. "There was only one more figure to put in place. We saved it for last, until I had finally completed my hypnodermic process. But last week Sam and I finished the job. With the addition of Smaug, it's done!"

Sam unexpectedly turned pink and stammered. "And it's a beautiful dragon, too! And it even expands with passion. But, unfortunately, I can't properly display my Smaug in public. I'm too shy. And besides, I'd get arrested."

While the crowd hooted, Sam spotted me, ogling in the front row, and winked at me, much to Bruno's chagrin. "Of course, I'm always amenable to private showings for the right person."

"You mean, a showing of your privates," Mike yelled out, starting the crowd up again. This time, it was my turn to do the Pink Lady bit. But I was grinning like a four-year-old who's just been promised a popsicle in July.

standing in the kitchen looking way out across the fields
you see a face in the window it's not real, it's not real

It was at that moment that a disheveled figure burst into the studio. "Don't trust that Bruno! He's up to no good!" Everyone's eyes turned to the intruder. "I got this skull on my arm last week." He ripped off his sleeve to show us. Purple and lurid, it seemed to pulse. "And I've had terrible headaches ever since. And bad thoughts. I've had to fight off the strangest urges. It's all I could do to stay sane this whole time. I know Bruno's responsible! Something isn't right – he's up to something. Don't trust him! I'm warning —" He broke off his diatribe when he spotted a fleshy freight train named Sam charging him from the stage. In a panic he turned on his heel and dashed out the door and down the street, with gorgeous Sam in hot pursuit, howling and cursing at his prey as he closed in upon him. "This swear we all: death we shall deal him ere Day's ending, woe unto world's end!"

The stranger didn't get far. We all watched in fascination, as Sam slammed him head-first against a wall and then began pounding him repeatedly with his ham-like fists and kneeing him with all the furious force he could muster. Before anyone could interfere, the man's face was a bloody pulp, one eye bulging from its socket. The Reverend with the bird on his back tried to intervene, but Sam shrugged him off, almost effortlessly. And we could all hear the SNAP when Sam jerked the man's chin from his neck. The sound brought Sam to his senses. He slumped to the ground and began bawling like a sudden widower.

No one moved until Bruno pushed his way from the back of the crowd. He kicked the prone stranger before kneeling beside Sam and put a big towel around his shoulders like a shawl. He cradled him in his lap until the police and ambulance arrived. The victim of Sam's attack lay bent and unmoving the entire time. He didn't even twitch.

I'm just standing in a doorway I'm just trying to make some sense

Shaken by the events that had transpired, I got home that night in time to turn on the news. I saw myself, ashen in the crowd, watching as the police escorted Sam, crying in handcuffs, into a patrol car and as an ambulance crew put a draped figure on a stretcher into their van. Bruno was gesticulating wildly to a cop who was taking notes on a pad. An attractive young reporter breathlessly recapitulated. "Sam Wise! Well-Known! In Our Community! For His Love Of The Greatest! Fantasy Novel Of Our Time! Has Been Charged! For The Brutal! Mauling! Death! Of Jimmy Hazelwood! An Unemployed Truck Driver!" Even though I had witnessed the chase and the beating, seeing it all on television again made it seem more real somehow. I felt sorry for Hazelwood and even sorrier for Sam. But to tell the truth, mostly I felt sorriest for myself and the lost Smaug. But that's life, I guess. I watched some zombie movie and went to bed. But I didn't sleep very well.

Strangely, over the next few days, I started seeing the people from the reception in the news as well.

Mike was found in his apartment with a self-inflicted bullet wound in his mouth. Friends who were interviewed claimed he had been depressed after his girlfriend had left him, but police were also investigating whether all of his clients' funds were safe. There were reports that they may have suddenly been transferred to unknown accounts.

On another night a photo of "Reverend Eagle" as I called him – I never got his name – flashed on the screen under the headline FUGITIVE FROM JUSTICE. "The Minister! Has Been Accused! Of Robbing! His Own Church!!! Of A Large Sum Of Money! Being Collected For A Bird Sanctuary At An Orphanage! And Disappearing With It! If Anyone! Knows His Whereabouts! Or The Location Of The Stolen Cash! Please Contact The Sheriff's Department! At The Phone Number Or E-Mail At The Bottom Of your Screen!"

Even Jerry and Brenda were being accused of committing arson against a series of tattoo parlors, though their whereabouts was still a mystery. This account in particular caught my attention. I was relieved to learn that L'INX had not been one of the targeted, because my own appointment was scheduled for the next day.

I showed up promptly at 10:00 in the morning. The décor had improved remarkably since the reception. There was new paint on the walls, new furniture; very attractive oil paintings instead of the old magazine cutout pictures of tattooed movie stars. Bruno, wearing a stylish new sweater and designer jeans, was waiting for me with a portfolio of butterflies, ankhs, and roses. "Or perhaps you'd like me to do a nice heart on your breast? It would give me a great deal of pleasure to do my best work there." But after some thought I knew what I wanted, in addition to the new watch of course. I insisted on an intricate pattern of Celtic and Arabesque chains on my forearms and ankles representing kismet and fatalism. "Maybe that is even more appropriate," Bruno agreed.

While he inked the design into my skin and sponged off the blood, Bruno seemed positively cheerful. He rattled on about how many years he had devoted to his new procedure and how it would enable him to achieve all the fantasies he had harbored since his youth. When he was done he made a clumsy pass at me, as I had anticipated, just like the first time he had worked on me. But this time, when I refused – with considerable heat on my part, I should add – he didn't seem to take my rejection too badly. An almost-smile even crossed his face and he just stared sort of dreamily at me as I left his parlor. "I'll see you again soon," he said.

Over the next few days, I guess due to all the stress from watching the dire fates of all my new friends on the news, I had severe migraines and insomnia. Shortly after midnight this morning, just to find some relief, I left home and drove around. Without paying much attention to the route I took, I found myself in Bruno's neighborhood. Seeing a light on in his parlor, I decided to see if he was in. I was surprised to find the front door open a crack, so I went in. I was even more surprised to see Bruno standing stark naked in the middle of his room.

He did not seem at all surprised by my entrance. Even more surprisingly, I actually started to disrobe. At first it was just a casual, automatic kind of action, like I was readying myself to go to bed after a long day at work, but by the time I had taken off my blouse I settled into a more rhythmic, undulating kind of vamp. And I became quite the tease, I tell you, as I slowly kicked off my shoes, one at a time, peeled off my stockings in a slow, sensuous motion, unhooked the snap on my skirt, and wriggled out of it after it fell to the floor.

Then I turned my back toward Bruno and undid my bra. Holding both ends to my side, with my arms crossed over my chest, I turned around again facing an open-mouthed Bruno. I allowed the bra to fall a bit and then pulled it back up, let it drop a little more, and brought it up again, repeating the action again and again until I saw Bruno begin to wet his lips. I briefly flashed one bare tit and immediately covered it again, and then the other, and then the bra was on the floor and I was cupping my hands over my nipples.

After some still moments I removed my fingers to my sides and stood there waving my upper torso to and fro like a seductive Bobo doll. (Actually, logically, shouldn't that be from and then to? I've always wondered about that.)

I stood there dancing in place, shaking my ass and tits a bit, and then I started to arch my back and move my butt farther and farther out. I put my thumb into my panties and pulled the waistband slightly off my stomach and put my right hand down on my crotch and started to rub myself as I began a low moan interrupted by an occasional squeak and intake of breath from Bruno.

By now, we were both licking our lips, though I hope I was doing it in a suggestive manner, because Bruno was salivating like Pavlov's doggie. And then I unrolled my panties down my gyrating, swiveling pelvis. Once again I turned around, and this time I shook my naked butt in Bruno's face. As he stretched his wriggling tongue toward my shivering buttocks I moved just beyond his reach, grabbed my panties with both hands and deftly tore them off. And then I turned again and stood stock still, waiting for Bruno to force himself on me.

Bruno was square in front of me, slack jawed, flaccid, his eyes squinched closed, his breath deep and irregular. After what seemed an eternity of facing off as bare as I was born but hairier in all the appropriate places I realized that Bruno was finished.

There would not be any fucking this night.

I dressed as quickly as I could and started out the door. "I'll see you again soon," I heard rasp out faintly behind me.

That prick. I never did like him. I left his place in disgust, relieved that he hadn't laid his hands on me and certainly pleased that he hadn't touched me with his disgusting little peter. But, all the same, I was humiliated. I had never been in a similar situation in which my partner had been so utterly unimaginative. Being naked with Bruno made me feel like a zombie – worse than that, in fact. Zombies were mindless automatons but I was fully conscious throughout though entirely unable to control my own actions. I never wanted to experience anything like that again.

But how would I ever be able to avoid it?. "I'll see you again soon." The events of the morning and of the past few weeks coalesced into a pattern: the free procedure, the news reports, the criminal activity. So I decided I have to look up the deranged bar code lady. I'm sure that anyone as paranoid as she is must have all sorts of guns and knives I can use.

But I'm standing here in the dawn without my clothes. And I still don't know if I'm supposed to use those tools against Bruno or against myself.

WE LUNATICS LOVE MARBLE POETS

we
are organized dust   ego constructed from cosmic mix   massproduced but with divergent faces   our destinies the crossings of expectation habit constitution accident   sculptors and poets waste their available dictionaries, unless resupplied by quarrymen and etymologists their arts would die on touch and tongue
lunatics
wanting the strength and beauty of youth we moon the sun   our fears defend the fortress while our foes search for our sally port   in dream we become vicious trees and randomic machines and thus think we are free from matter's fetters   the earth is my floorboard the sun my incandescent bulb   rains and rains (repetitions of repetitions) massage a hollow in the rock
love
an infinite latitude looking for a longitude to fix its place   each lover an assemblage of unlike entities, each an infinite diversity   an eventual child of memory doing that old mortar-and-pestle   our tears were blushes once   the wool outvalues the sheep, the horn its rhino
marble
no bowel no brain no brawn no breath   condemned to be free, slave stone accomplice of master sculptor   mutated by love by language by law by belief its appearance mirrors its butcher's thought   but it holds its is its was its will be   the sculpture never forgives the chisel
poets
try to keep secret the genius of their creation by gloving fingers and genitals but hints always reveal their command   juggling invisible maracas in nets of intimate timpani   imagination corrals disorder   complexity camouflages simplicity

ORIGAMI

A fold or fissure in the genes
decides if peacock or pigeon.
The origami of species
doomed Uncle Australopithecus.
The universe holds many its
and also all their opposites.
There's a temple in the brothel
and a brothel in the temple.

RUBICON

Each dawn comes embarrassed.
Time rearranges us, from chaos to chaos.

Our memories are ghosts of what
were once our pasts
before structures collapsed.

Infinities of if permit change to exist.
Wisdom becomes mischief.
Stoics become criers in meditation choirs for umbilical pyres.

Even the Rubicon once got lost in the swamps
and then was retro-conned.
Destiny is not fact.

Fates are carefully stacked by gambling architects
to construct poker fraud. Certainty's a façade,
installed by clever gods. Time rearranges us.

From chaos to chaos, each dawn comes embarrassed.

THE OBSCURITY OF HEAVEN

The bomb is in the temple, the eraser on the page.
Our timid mirrors reflect but they never take a step.
A cancer's in the nipple, spectators usurp the stage.

The clouds as integral as stars (as heaven's measured from Earth)
And we moan that circumstance proves to be our best defense.
We mourn heaven: "It's obscured, so we cannot know its worth."

Our judgment misjudges us and aborts our renaissance.
We can reject starvation without accepting poison.
The body discharges pus while mitigating relapse.

Hunkering down in our forts is desperate strategy.
To drive the enemy back we must go upon attack.
Garret verse, a poet's corpse that has no utility.

WHAT ABOUT THE AGE OF LOVERS?

The age of heroes is broken.
The palace is now aflame.
Historians' age is growing.

The heroes are not to blame,
for, though their strength is diminished
it isn't demolished yet.
Tomorrow's the resurrection
but today is just a rest.

Our bodies and experience
form the borders of our mind.
But there exists That Beyond Sense
that we cannot understand.

We get confused in worlds not right.
If bandit's in the library
and pundit's gloved at the prize fight
we can't tell steppes from prairies.
We imagine a symmetry
that we cannot yet define.

We assign all our mysteries
to God, to magic, to time.

We gird our egos in armor
to weaken our defenses,
but freedom embraces karma,
aggression joins resistance.
Desire develops into deed.
Our matches become beacons.

We were waves that became a sea
and rowboats that grew riggings.

Orators are clothed in words
and scholars stand on language.
But heroes must speak through their work
and lovers through their anguish.

UNAPPRECIATED GIFTS

We act dreams, sleep science.
Futures wait to be opened.
Pasts are already broken.
Newborns clutch their fists and cry,
open-palmed dead are quiet.
Instants between are presents.

As we stumble through ourselves,
our parasites and our priests,
our magistrates and our thieves,
our streetcorner disciples
handing out little bibles….

We must occupy them all.

TIMES AS GOLDEN CALVES

All the pasts have their futures
and all futures have their pasts.
But the present is itself.
Plaster casts and black sutures
cohabit with surgeons' masks. Doctors lift up their scalpel like an execution axe in service of ice sculptors. They daydream of parachutes to hurtle them through their clouds.

And the butcher is carcass,
as the treaty is the war, as the poacher is his traps. The scarecrow loves the crow, and the shooter shares the blast. Ventriloquist is dummy when a be stops becoming.

Views of peasant and castle
once framed the common outlook, as though sheep needed the wolves, as though serfs needed dukes, to justify how a gulf would link prey to predator by way of divine order.

SIGNS

The philosophers,
poets, and scholars,
workers of the mind,
invented Mankind.

They made Being firm
by creating terms
and categories,
those mythic stories,
right words and patterns,

shaped God as Saturn,
then as mere planet —

Elements – Senates —
Beauty – Inch – Language —
Society – Beige —
History — Prisms —
Patriotism —
Sin – Geography –
Self – Heredity —
Time — The Unconscious.....

The list is endless.

These concepts define
our world by their signs.

A symbol's an is
that's also an else.

FIX

Not by any charms or karma,
we all are ruled by lips and arms.
The best arms are kept under sleeve—
phantom limbs we almost believe.
Lips must always be in action:
proclamations propaganda
posters slogans podcasts broadsides
downloads headlines broadcasts soundbites
to entertain alarm arouse
justify distract and excuse.
Terrorists! Fascists! Immigrants
Steal Our Land Our Jobs Our Women!
Innies! Outies! Leftists! Righties!
Liberals! Mobs! Neo Nazis!
Prosperity Or Poverty!
Our Freedom Or Our Slavery!
Criminals! Our Open Borders!
Infidels! Monarchists! Trade War!
Stolen Elections! Deviants!
Antisemites! Spies! Jacobins!
Family Values! Lies! Misfits!
Epidemics! Nuclear Threats!
Divine Order! Thieves! Bolsheviks!
And thus we're judased by a fix.

... RAW OF THE ROSES ...

a

When we played at being young
we were all less old than raw
All were hangers, none were hanged
and all were knights of the Lord

And then the ordered murder
that joins the chaos of raw
succeeded the disorder
that normalized our Before

Our invisible missiles
and markless wounds from the raw
advanced to marches and drills
medals formations and corps
the glory and brotherhood
the backwardness of raw
the salute to blood and mud
and boredom broken by gore

Our red company carries
symbol standards of our raw
spear and aegis of ares
forged by the hammer of thor

b

it was one hundred years raw ...
raw of spanish succession ...
that great patriotic raw ...
trojan ... peloponnesian ...

pastry raw ... pig raw ... kettle
raw ... or the whiskey rebellion ...
or la guerra del fútbol ...
afghan raw ... jinshin-no-ran

guerra de pacífico ...
or la guerre des trois henri ...
crusades ... bello gallico...
or the raw of jenkins ear ...

raw of the oranges ... the straits ...
in the mahābhārata ...
opium raw ... the eight saints ...
or the raw of the stray dog ...

GAZA REDUX

This time there is no honey left in the lion
and there are no brass shackles on Samson.
Arise, mace and chariot of Dagon!

Trouble began when mythical brothers
confused their identities as others'
shadows and mirrors, instead of doubles.

Dagon resented the enemy's reign.
Injustice and neglect made him insane.
"They've laid waste our land and multiplied our slain."

Nova morning burst and then exploded.
Nova dancers flared up and then went dead.
The sun worshipers fled while others bled.

Samson was ordered to regrow his mane
and to resume his judgment, now unchained,
and yet remain blind to the others' pain.

The jawbone of an ass – heartless orders —
Samson deploys 30-cubit shoulders —
the heaps upon heaps of children smolder.

Samson expands an eye for an eye
to peacock's tails and needles' eyes.
Gaza is as flax that was burnt with fire.

Burn all the wells! Keep the corpses hostage!
Grind up humanity into sausage:
tabulate but don't value the lossage.

Samson/Dagon said: "Though you have done this,"
(each said) "yet of you will I be avenged
and after that" (they promised) "I will cease."

Samson said, "Now shall I be more blameless,
though" (Dagon said) "I do them displeasure
to do to him as he hath done to me."

Soldiers and martyrs measure their service
on the basis of duties, not mercies.
Each world regards the world as its world is.

TIME MACHINE

Echoless laughter
marked the mocking
rictor sardonicus
of our love,

showing us that time
is the machine
that shredshredshreds presents
into pasts.

And tomorrow's rich
tapestries, which
were infinite once, have
slimmed to threads.

Life's chaos indeed
is orderly but
not in ways we have
deciphered.

Our universe was
not Galileo's
and also won't be
our children's,

but all their loves and
all their changes
will still be all the same
probably.

ARCHITECTURES DECAY

Thus, age bleeds away youth and turns dentures into lace.
The taut drum of your skin becomes a worn stocking,
untoned, crumpled, and thin. Winter freeze bruises fruit,
your garden becomes waste, and those grim burlap bags
that hang from those pegs were once blimps that flew flags
all were pleased to salute. Monuments get defaced.

THE DANCE: NANCY

I said I wouldn't dance with you:
Your hair's too blonde, your eyes too blue.
A loaded gun and fully cocked,
dynamite cap set to go off.
I swore I wouldn't dance with you.

She's too proud of humility.
Her giant modesty towers from her knees.
She's so proud of humility, the giant Modesty towers from her knees.
Even us healthy ones she treats like disease.

I said I wouldn't dance with you.
Your arms, I knew, would hold like glue.
No neon ever hijacked us,
I refused to be target practice.
I knew I'd never dance with you.

Oversharp in her ignorance, she's
indisputably a genius between the knees.
Oversharp in her ignorance, undeniably she's a genius between her knees.
The peacock preens, pretending that no one sees.

I said I wouldn't dance with you:
The night's too young, too bright's the view.
But that bandit moon lit the fuse,
and insurgent night made the news,
though I'd said I'd never dance with you,

dancing in the moon
light with Nancy and kissing her good —
Night
comes quickly this time of year
and icily as well: the wind
bites nicely and to the quick—
oh these thoughts! are dancing nicely
through the wind kissing this memory
somehow – I can hear the

memory embers
hisssing in the wind (is sharp
this time of year) like java in the night
comes dark and sharp and bitter.
Spring it was or was it fall? (no matter)
(no matter at all the season) the reason
I recall at all is Nancy her name
whispers in the moon light, or
is it the night
wind that's light
or was it the fall —
— no matter —
it was time and she was mine and we were
hours until the dawn (comes quickly, this time)
and I must go on
I wanted to go on, to bound
fast as the hound Wind
and as free too but I was bound too fast to the ground
and ground too far down and
ground far too fine too but I danced on
with Nancy till I was out of time
and out of mind (but I must go on for now)
I dance with my mind I dance
with the wind and the night and the ice and
but where is the Nancy?
I dance with memory and death and death and memory
and now the dancing's through, for
every spring one makes, a fall's not far behind—
and life and mind and night and wind
go quickly this year of time and mightily as well
and all matter
(but no matter)
though I promised never to dance with you.

Most of fame is a lie

UNPARALLELED LIVES

1. The Stories That Keep Me Saved

From ocean to bush
to mountain to sea
Beelzebub and Zeus
are chasing after me.
One promises fire,
and one, lightning bolts.
They want my surrender,
they want me to convert
my riches to embers
that will die in the dirt.
I love the burning bush
that walked upon the sea,

Adam's figs and apples,
Eve's frankincense and myrrh,
Baptist's tabernacle,
Delilah's virgin birth.
Ark of Harold Angels
sinks in the lotus pond
while the lamb and Daniel
wait in the lion's den.

Grafitti at the feast
that read, "Thigh Kingdom Come."
Magis from the east,
their whore from Babylon,
the ones who suffered
when the Pharaoh Joseph
devoured the golden calf
during the last supper
ahead of Jonah's flood.
Peter and his bishops,
when the wine turned to blood,
stole the leaves and fishes.

Allah-lujah Rama Christos Amen Om

2. Barabbas and Jesus

Barabbas and Jesus
out walking in the sands
and along comes Pilate
wanting to wash his hands.

"Hey, Boss, why you so cross?"
the good Barabbas said.
Replied Pilate, "Herod!
John Baptist gave him head!"

"How mean!" said Magdalene,
"Intruding on my job!"
Pilate: "Please understand,"
(rehearsing for the mob)

"someone must take the brunt,
it's me or one of you."
Barabbas thought then said
"Will nailing two thieves do?"

And Pilate said "My guy!
Indeed, that may suffice."
But then they heard Peter's
cock. It crowed only twice.

And Jesus wept. "The jig
is up. I'll see you soon.
First I must meet Judas
at the Last Chance Saloon."

3. Sacrifices, All

Oh, those gladiolas
that brightened Pilate's halls,
like his gladiators,
distractions from trials.

A pilot brags about
the size of his payload
and he forgets about
chasing some horizon.
He imagines himself
to be a volcano.
Will you permit yourself,
then, to be the virgin?

4. Agitprop

Topiarists shape the grayed seeds in our tender plants. They organize our dust, though we notice not. The stilted ladies in their paint, and the cops they pretend to date. The Tower of Books and the Ghost's Magic Shell; a sleeping warren and an ambitious vice enable the Dulles Dallas murder *omertà*. The million-dollar broker lads caught green in their bachelor pads. Lazy and late, we lose ourselves in steeled canyons and concrete caverns. The nurses in the underground. Scourge and scorpions lurk everywhere. The old pianist in the lounge trying to woo the aloof barkeep, who thinks the player's a creep. We run in quiet into the libraries of the dead. The judges, wise in their docket, fondling bullets in their pockets. In their ritualistic masturbation, historians conjure up our heroes. The mafioso in the church reserving usage of its hearse. Our yesterdays are already mummies, disemboweled and embalmed, but tomorrow's resurrection is an optimist's myth. Singing priest seeking martyrdom willing to settle for stardom. Beauty, safety, and utility are the propagandas civilization uses to excuse itself.

5. Menagerie in E Major

The monk cast that day's third I-Ching
and then he made his turkey sing
to entertain the drunk heathens.
And the Turk had his monkey dance
in his red sequined funky pants.
The monk's turkey and Turk's monkey
showed them both they were worth money,
so Monk and the Turk joined forces
and purchased two purloined horses
that they taught to play bass and drums.
They toured as The Amazing Ones,
led by a jazzy pachyderm
who blew triumphant saxophone.

6. "The Body's Guest"

Though Sir Walter was a poet and knight
he never learned to spell his surname right.

[He is not known to have ever used the Raleigh spelling. In 1578 he was Rawleyghe (though on the same deed his father was Ralegh and his brother was Rawlygh). He also signed himself as Raleghe and Rauleigh. But until 1583 he was mostly Rauley; in that year, when he was about 31, he finally became Ralegh, though briefly he reverted to Rauley. James VI of Scotland referred to him as Raulie; William Cecil as Rawly, and his son Robert as Rawley, and Robert's secretary as Raweley and Rawlegh. The Privy Council wrote of Rawleighe, and Rawleigh. Otherwise he was Raghley Raghlie Raileig, Raileghe Raleagh Raley Raleye Raleygh Raleyghe Raligh Ralighe Rallegh Ralleigh Ralli Raughleye Raughlie Raughleigh Raugleighe Raugleugh Raughly Raule Rauleghe Rauleighe Raulghe Raulighe Rauly Raulyghe Raweleigh Rawely Rawlee Rawlei Rawleie Rawleye Rawleygh Rawlie Rawliegh Rawlighe Rawlye Rawlyghe Raylie Raylye Raylygh Reigley Rhaleigh Rhaley Rhaly Rolye Wrawley and even Wrawly. And these were how his English associates referred to him! Foreigners called him Rale Raleghus Ralego Raleich Raleik Ralle Rallé Raulaeus Real Reali and Rhalegh. James ascended the English throne as James I and, upon meeting the famous knight, remarked to him, "I have heard rawly of thee" and had him executed.]

7. Ease or Life: An Ideological Divide between Left and Right, 1776

"Ease. Liberty.
Happiness."
—Adam Smith,
economist:
WEALTH OF NATIONS,

"Life. Liberty.
Pursuit of Happiness."
—Jefferson,
utopian:
DECLARATION

In their efforts to understand the conditions of liberty and a possibility of happiness to some degree, presupposing life or ease, two thinkers invoked a hidden hand in their formulaic diptych: Creator or Market – which? One slogan was fundamental, and one, developmental.

8. Silent Immortality

Time has translated Sappho into silence.
Her soundless poems, invisible to the ear,
echo in imagination and amnesia.
Impervious to changing fashion,
invulnerable against critics.

9. Paris Erection

His cock had set the hour
when Paris' city would die.

Eiffel made a tower
to mate Paris with the sky.

10. The Great

Macedon's Alexander
born in myrrh, died in velvet
lived as verb, lived as helmet
Babylon's fatal pander

11. Richard First

Across geographies,
maintaining emperors
by cults and soldiery

has been a commonplace
matter of procedure
against the populace.

Richard had good PR—
yes, he was popular
among the troubadours.

And today, presidents
who can stay in power
are loved by journalists.

12. When Davy Crockett Went Down

For two weeks
188 Texans
beat off
over two thousand Mexicans.

And that is why we remember
the Alamo.

13. That Clinton Administration

A youthful intern named Monica
celebrated that year's Hanukkah
by performing for her boss.
He gave her dreidel a toss
and then she played his harmonica.

14. The Hurrians

Now our bodies are museums
and our faces are atlases.
The metropolis that hastened
from the joints of our hemispheres
still hymn and jump and hosanna,
but, hushed too soon, they all will rush
to meet us in the common ash.
Fado fades into atmosphere.

15. Carnival of Love

The bearded lady
has two lovers,
the apeman and the geek.

Their sex is crazy,
peeling rubber
on high wires and the street.

When bearded lady
becomes mother
to a new circus freak,

the lucky baby
has two others
to help him feel unique.

16. Joint Maneuvers

Di dandles her tea like any grande dame
and she handles her whiskey as well
as a man.

I was a sergeant in the cavaliers.
I prized my targets
and my bandoleer,
my spurs
and my plume.
A chest of medals occupied
my room, none claimed in battle.

Di was a waitress.
She wanted to stop pretending princess
and
       rise to the
              top.
One with ambition seeks one with regret.
"To starve the kitchen, feed a cook's credit."

One day when marching my tattoos
and flutes,
my eyes kept watching Di's
bonnet and boots.
My parade dismissed,
this hungry soldier,
Sir Knight on a quest,
double-timed over to where she still stood.

As fierce
and as free
as fire from a woods,
Di saluted me
with crisp precision.

I saluted her back
stiff at attention—
never felt the flak
    exploding
inside.

The wounded man
wed the ambushing bride.

And I never fled
the combat that came.
My new purple heart
marked my
rise to fame
and Di's
state of art.

As I rose in rank it was her mission
to protect my flank and her position.
One with ambition
needs one with regret.
"To starve the kitchen, feed a cook's credit."

Di's deft riding crop
urges her stallion to boldly gallop
beyond battalions.

17. Francis Drake

My hands are caked and yours are so fine,
but somehow they fit
trim together like ships of the line.
Marry me, oh carry me, sign your name mine:
I'll be Francis Drake and you'll be my *Golden Hind*.
I'll fill up your hold with all of the gold
that I can find, all of the gold that I can find.

We'll dance naked, if you're so inclined —
just billow our charms,
wrap our sheets round yardarms entwined.
I'll ride you oh I'll guide you, make your name shine.
I'll be Francis Drake and you'll be my *Golden Hind*.
I'll fill up your hold with all of the gold that I can find.
I'll fill up your hold with all of the gold,
with all of the gold,
with all of the gold
that I can find.

I'll be Francis Drake and you'll be my *Golden Hind*.

18. Inheritants

It was Adam's first sunset.

Clothed fully in nakedness
he watched blush balance blackness
and studied how the ruby
became coal-dull and sooty.

He was the man of duty;
thus Moses would brand Adam;
Paul would call him the pattern.

We are cuttings from his garden.

Eve's limbs sprawled cloudward. She lay
there like an uprooted tree.
"Bury us, we are the seeds."

We still pray for redemption,
never for reconstruction.

So, when all is said and done,
immortal Adam and Eve,
our pools carry your dead leaves
and we echo you always.

THE STATE OF THE LAW

Justice is just a corpse
the surgeon said
and she died when she lost her soul
No, she lives, but a whore
the virgin said
since her favors are bought with gold
so your lawbooks are porn
this urchin says
which obituaries enfold

TRINITY

Sometimes there are times when
the princess is the dragon
and other times, the hero.

Ego/id/superego
function together, one engine.

Three Norns knot the same emblem
for us all – Win, Lose, and Draw —
worn by the ménage à trois
called HolyghostFatherSon,
a universal slogan.

GENETIC MAGI

None of us are children of virgins,
we are offspring of love and need.

And at the cross of dream and burden
we draw our ration of the blood and seed.

The happy lattices of our bones
organize the ivies of our flesh,
the joiners of the mangers and thrones
create the monument and the niche
that link our baptisms and our graves.
Our architecture is our haven.

Lives vibrate between playgrounds and plagues,
waver from danger to salvation.

WHERE DO THESE, OUR CASTRATI, GO?

On the march—
the rag, the drum, the bugle's linger.
In the church—
the wine, the crumb, the seedless singer.
By the curb—
the road, the thumb, sundrunk and cindered.

Remnants of sacrificial souls.

Hurricane cuddles eye

CENOZOIC

Dinosaurs didn't stay
dinosaurs, did they?
They became chickens
and museum exhibitions.

What about us?
Hitchhikers once,
between exits,
and not yet fixed
to this landscape
of no escape.

LOOK AT THESE STREETS: THEY'RE MUSIC.
THE LINES, THE SHADOWS, CRYING OUT MELODIES
   —Lance Tait

The traffic cadence hymned as muggers rapped and scored.
Ambulance sopranos sang and danced till morrow
and lovers took encores. The magic never dimmed.

SUBURBAN SHOESTORE

So, you inhabit a steady orbit,
you're comfortable – or, that is, until
chaos comet comes. Not on provisions
have you spent your self, but on emptied shelves.
You paid prostitutes to wear all the boots.

FOWL WEATHER

Six ducks in a pond
swimming through a warm sweet spring rain—
pond is duck is air.

METAMORPHOSIS

Brave audience caterpillar
agrees to enter
the stage magician's magic box—

NIGHT SHIFT

Last night I studied the sky from my porch,
Suddenly an ignited cosmic torch
burned and slashed through Cancer.
Even though I know my constellations
I continue to have doubts and questions,
since I doubt stars have the answers,

You, modeler of phases of my moon,
did you watch that spectacle from your room?
Our sections of the sky don't quite rhyme,
our eternities look like different
patterns of buckshot in a canvas tent.
Whose Heaven's bigger, yours or mine?

WEATHER REPORT FOR BLIND OPTIMISTS

Proudly, dawn brings out
those debutante clouds of swan —
black vultures
are secluded
from this slack culture,
tragedy is outlawed
from all our strategies.

Gradually, stratosphere turns lapis lazuli.

OLD SONGS SUNG AGAIN

This beach that we run on, this beach that we sun on,
was a cold mountain once, indomitable quartz.
An insatiable wind chewed the granite into flinders.
The weathered remains gathered themselves as grains
along this treasured shore, this diamond corridor.
But the bored, restless waves too soon will take their leave,
Our beach's secret cache will be revealed: the smashed
shells, patches of lather, condoms, crap, cadavers….

Life is like a ledger book.
Plusses and losses shape our plans.

The past is a castle; the present, a pasture:
Both are famous for blades (for cattle, or for knaves).
Instants leave instantly, last an eternity,
and new historians find and restore eons.
…. Mississippi …. Egypt …. Pasts clatter in their crypts,
yesterday's tomorrows detached from their augurs.

Busses and crosses map our lands.
Life deserves a second look.

UNKNOTTED

Far off we see those bright quasars
captured by their own black holes,
their old buds dying inside,
hopes fettered to fears,
guards shackled to their convicts.

We're soft diamonds under iron skies.
Lovers of the youth earth's noises,
but raised in cold and shady nations
where light is unknotted from the sun,
we end here in ancient silence.

BODY AND SELF

To deflesh,
the shaman,
the seer,
the mystic
lacerates,
purges,
starves,
punishes,
isolates
the body
of the self.

The poet,
inventor,
entrepreneur
concentrates
the body
of the self
on the solution
of a problem
like a laser
microscope,
to deflesh.

An ordinary,
to deflesh,
removes from
the flesh
of the body
by reading,
by dreaming,
by jogging,
by gaming,
by giving,
by loving.

SANCTIFIED

Impatient to cohabit,
the shot in the hunter's gun
and his *fiancée* rabbit
rendezvous in the red dawn.

This sacrament of union
consecrates nature's sabbath.

The 10th-generation nun
inherited the habits
of her ever-gracious mom
and that unchastened abbott.

They celebrate the sabbaths
and god honors the unions.

TOWARDS A SMALL PLOT

Gilt and brocaded mahogany room
in shadow. Windowed by assassins moon.

Seated, pinkie-ringed consiglieri
filling his function as emissary
furthering the aims of his fireworks king—
smooth ambassador equipped with a sting.

Apocalyptic fanfare and flourishes.

Enter empress creole from Mauritius.
Watercolor face, manicured perfume.

"Greetings to you, my friend." "Greetings to you."

And then they proceed to philosophize
on how life is defined by how it dies,
a brief discourse on poisons and daggers.
"Which do you prefer? Frozen or staggered?"

They make their pact, reach terms on a contract,
which leads to a series of traps and acts....

[But circumstances shifted and altered
and she armored her intended target.
Volcanoes consolidate to islands,
and ocean motions erode these to sand.]

ON HUMAN ADAPTATION TO HARSH HABITATS

If you've imagined
vast sandy ruins
you should intuit
there are Bedouins.
And icy wastelands
would seem to imply
there are Inuit
who would there reside.

HOW TO SUCCEED AT DAIRY FARMING (AND OTHER PURSUITS)

Like a lover, like a boss,
the cow gives the sweetest milk
when caressed,
when gently stroked.

THE LANGUAGE I USE ABROAD

I belong to an organization of debates
between inner and outer genitals.
The members meet on a regular basis
to engage in intercourse
and exchange positions.
When English fails to persuade
I rely on Gesture and Patience.

FIT AND PROPER

Oohs and aahhs
are appropriate
for fireworks
horoscopes
and massages

but sunsets —
anniversaries —
wakes – deserve
some respect.

Admiral
or boatswain
— promotion's
admirable.

But we neglect
to honor
the farmers —
mechanics —
the steady.

FISHING WITH A LINGUIST

I never claimed my German was good
but I can conjugate worm and hook,
and I can understand your language
by knowing of your hopes and anguish,
of your cathedrals and your ruins.
We all communicate in Human.
I'm not fluent in Russian or Greek,
but I practice my Reason and Grace.

DECREATION

It is one moment past midnight
on the 8th day of morning.

Our Styx ferries become consumed
with the burning of bibles.

Seven heavens eighten themselves
and shrink and infinitize.

In this silent Babel
the sciencemagic we learned
while head over heels upside down
from hanged Marut and Harut
is finding and losing its feet.

Apocalypse collapses.
Ahuramazda unities
vanish darkness into bright.

Medusa's pale horse Pegasus
comets Quetzalcoatl;
Fenris swallows the Eighth Archon
and then pukes and pukes him out.

The set sun eludes prediction.
No west exists to rise from.

WE GAMBLERS OF FATE ARE PLAYED BY THE JUGGLERS OF TIME

The silence of echoes is too loud to hear.
The excess deer were culled
before the hunt was closed.
We race toward that precipice we screened ourselves from.
Lazarus' miracle
just delayed the dust.
We are partners of the same condition.
Though odds up and fall
our lots have been tossed.
The future always lies to us, but so does the past.

You get the apple
filling – You get the crust.
Paths twist and twist no matter which we pick.
You get the pedestal—
and You get the bust.
Rivers have many tributaries but only one result.
You get the sadist's fuel,
You the holocaust.

www.ingramcontent.com/pod-product-compliance
Lightning Source LLC
Chambersburg PA
CBHW081429070526
44586CB00020B/2533